Flash Portuguese

PAULO
FEYTOR
PINTO

EMPRESA PROMOTORA
DA LÍNGUA PORTUGUESA

A **Lidel** adquiriu este estatuto através da assinatura de um protocolo com o **Camões - Instituto da Cooperação e da Língua,** que visa destacar um conjunto de entidades que contribuem para a promoção internacional da língua portuguesa.

EDIÇÃO E DISTRIBUIÇÃO
Lidel – Edições Técnicas, Lda.
Rua D. Estefânia, 183, r/c Dto. – 1049-057 Lisboa
Tel.: +351 213 511 448
lidel@lidel.pt
Projetos de edição: editoriais@lidel.pt
www.lidel.pt

LIVRARIA
Av. Praia da Vitória, 14 A – 1000-247 Lisboa
Tel.: +351 213 511 448
livraria@lidel.pt

Copyright © 2019, Lidel – Edições Técnicas, Lda.
ISBN edição impressa: 978-972-757-711-8
1.ª edição impressa: junho 2019

Conceção de *layout*: José Manuel Reis
Paginação: Pedro Santos
Impressão e acabamento: Tipografia Lousanense, Lda. – Lousã
Depósito Legal: 456686/19

Capa: José Manuel Reis

Créditos das imagens: página 112 ©Luso; página 114 ©svetavo, ©nd700, © kieferpix, ©elena_larina, ©valentinarr, ©uckyo, ©white78, ©Cucu Remus; página 116 @Magone; página 143 ©clu; página 147 ©PenWin.

Todos os nossos livros passam por um rigoroso controlo de qualidade, no entanto, aconselhamos a consulta periódica do nosso *site* (www.lidel.pt) para fazer o *download* de eventuais correções.

Contents

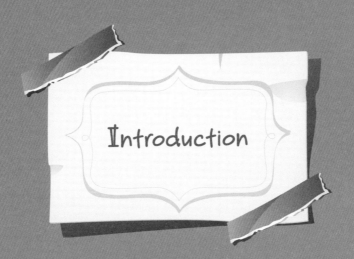

Introduction

Let us make it clear right from the beginning: with this book, you will never get to perfectly understand and make yourself understood in Portuguese. Hopefully, though, you will quickly be able to understand and make yourself understood in most situations you are likely to experience while in Portugal.

However, this is different from a phrasebook. There are no endless lists of phrases and sentences for you to learn by heart. We would rather give you the very basic tools for you to build up your own speaking skills. Of course, you will always have to remember the vocabulary and some rules. To make your life easier, we will use what you likely know about English and also consider the fact that you might speak English but actually have a different mother tongue.

Because the idea is for you to 'mingle with Portuguese', we will give you loads of background and context info so you can learn more about the country and its people beyond words, phrases, and expressions. Although this book focuses on the mother tongue of the majority of the people living in Portugal, you will also find reference to other languages spoken in the country. English, for example!

Warm Up

English words used in Portuguese
Palavras inglesas usadas em português

English words of Portuguese origin
Palavras inglesas de origem portuguesa

Portuguese words of English origin
Palavras portuguesas de origem inglesa

Portuguese names of foreign cities
Nomes portugueses de cidades estrangeiras

Other Portuguese words of foreign origin
Outras palavras portuguesas de origem estrangeira

ENGLISH WORDS USED IN PORTUGUESE

BACON

BACKGROUND

BESTSELLER

COCKTAIL

DOWNLOAD

COWBOY

FEEDBACK

FLASH

MARKETING

JAZZ

ENGLISH WORDS OF PORTUGUESE ORIGIN

ALBATROSS

alcatraz, pelican<*al-ghattâs* (Arabic), diver. The English word was first registered in the 17th century and would come back to Portuguese in the 19th century as *albatroz*, the word currently used.

BAMBOO

bambu<*bambu* (Marathi, India).

BAROQUE

barroco, clayish<*barro*, clay. *Barroco*, a qualifier, was first used in the feminine expression *pérola barroca*, clayish pearl, irregular pearl as if made out of clay like the baroque shapes, irregular when compared to previous classical style.

CASHEW

caju<*aka'yu* (Tupi, Brazil).

COBRA

cobra, any snake including cobra.

FETISH

feitiço, witchcraft, spell. *Feitiço* became *fétiche* in French and *fetish* in English in the 17th century. In the late 19th century, it came back to Portuguese, from French. Currently, the Portuguese use both words: *feitiço* (witchcraft, spell) and *fetiche* (worshiped object).

MANDARIN

mandarim<*mattari* (Malay), counsellor+*mandar* (Portuguese), to command.

MANGO

manga<*manga* (Malayalam, India).

MARMALADE

marmelada, quince jam<*marmelo*, quince. *Marmelada* is also slang for having sex. It appears that in the distant past quince was considered an aphrodisiac.

MOLASSES

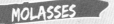

melaço, honeyish<*mel*, honey.

PORTUGUESE WORDS OF ENGLISH ORIGIN

BIFE beef, but meaning any steak

CHAMPÔ shampoo

CLUBE club

COMPUTADOR computer

FUTEBOL football

IMPLEMENTAR to implement

LANCHE lunch, but meaning evening tea, mid-afternoon snack

PUDIM pudding

LÍDER leader

RALI rally, but meaning only car race

PORTUGUESE NAMES OF FOREIGN CITIES

AMESTERDÃO Amsterdam

SEVILHA Sevilla

ANTUÉRPIA Antwerpen

TEERÃO Tehrān

ESTOCOLMO Stockholm

TURIM Torino

GENEBRA Genève

XANGAI Shàng Hǎi

MUNIQUE München

NOVA IORQUE New York

BACALHAU *kabeljau* (Dutch), cod

BATUQUE *batchuk* (Xironga, Mozambique), drum

BILHETE *billet* (French), ticket

BIOMBO *biôbu* (Japanese), screen

BUÉ *bwe* (Kimbundu, Angola), slang for very, or many

CEDILHA *zedilla* (Spanish), small comma sign in letter ç

CHÁ *ch'a* (Mandarin), tea

CONVITE *convit* (Catalan, Spain), invitation

GAJO *gadjo* (Romani), slang for guy

SAPO *apo* (Basque, Spain), toad

Context

Languages in the 13th century
Línguas no século XIII

Portuguese accents
Sotaques portugueses

Other mother tongues
Outras línguas maternas

Portuguese attitudes towards languages
Atitudes dos Portugueses perante as línguas

LANGUAGES IN THE 13TH CENTURY

Alcañices
1297

Chaves
1231

Leonés

Galego
Português

Francês

Francês

Moçárabe Ocidental
e
Árabe Ibérico

Faro
1249

▷ The Northern border has been stable since Chaves became permanently Portuguese (1231).

▷ The Southern border has been stable since Faro became Portuguese (1249).

▷ The Eastern border has been (more or less) stable since the Treaty of Alcañices (1297).

▷ Portuguese Galician was the Portuguese or Southern variety of Galician spoken all over Northwestern Iberia. First known record from 1175.

▷ Leonese was the Latin language from the neighbouring kingdom of Leon, spoken in an area spanning from Asturias to Spanish Extremadura.

▷ French was spoken by many ex-crusaders and other French settlers. The father of the first king of Portugal was a crusader himself, from Burgundy.

▷ Western Mozarabic was the local variety of the Latin language spoken by Christians in Southern Iberia under Islamic rule.

▷ Iberian Arabic was the Iberian variety of Arabic spoken mainly in towns and cities since the 8th century.

▷ Hebrew, the written language of the growing Jewish community.

▷ Latin was the declining written language of religion and knowledge.

▷ Around the 14th century, Portuguese Galician and Western Mozarabic had already merged into Portuguese, the language of all legal texts. By the 18th century, mainly because of the Inquisition, Portugal had become a country with one religion, one culture and one language.

EUROPEAN PORTUGUESE ACCENTS

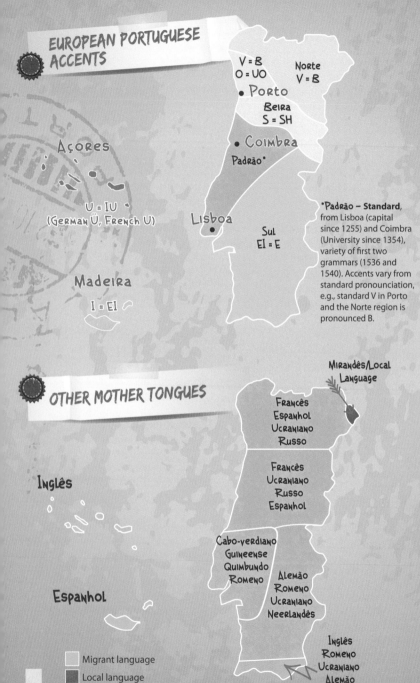

V = B
O = UO

Norte
V = B

• Porto

Beira
S = SH

• Coimbra

Padrão*

Açores

U = IU
(German Ü, French U)

Lisboa

Sul
EI = E

Madeira

I = EI

*Padrão – Standard, from Lisboa (capital since 1255) and Coimbra (University since 1354), variety of first two grammars (1536 and 1540). Accents vary from standard pronounciation, e.g., standard V in Porto and the Norte region is pronounced B.

OTHER MOTHER TONGUES

Mirandês/Local Language

Francês
Espanhol
Ucraniano
Russo

Inglês

Francês
Ucraniano
Russo
Espanhol

Cabo-verdiano
Guineense
Quimbundo
Romeno

Alemão
Romeno
Ucraniano
Neerlandês

Espanhol

Inglês
Romeno
Ucraniano
Alemão

Migrant language
Local language

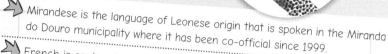

Around 2% of the population speaks Brazilian Portuguese.

➤ Mirandese is the language of Leonese origin that is spoken in the Miranda do Douro municipality where it has been co-official since 1999.

➤ French is spoken by ex-migrants in France, returned after 1974. Every Summer, in August, it is the most widely spoken language in rural areas of the North and Centre.

➤ Spanish is spoken by ex-migrants in Venezuela and Spanish professionals.

➤ Ukrainian is spoken by workers arrived after 1998.

➤ Russian is spoken by workers arrived after 1998.

➤ Capeverdean creole is the most widespread minority language, spoken by 1% of the general population. It is a creole type based on 15th and 16th centuries Portuguese vocabulary.

➤ Bissau-Guinean creole is based on 15th and 16th centuries Portuguese vocabulary and mother tongues of workers arrived after 1974.

➤ Kimbundu is a Bantu language from Angola, spoken by workers and expatriates arrived after 1974.

➤ German and Dutch are the mother tongues of expatriates and tourists.

➤ English is the mother tongue of expatriates and tourists. In the Azores it is spoken by ex-migrants in the U.S.

➤ Romanian is spoken by workers arrived after 1998.

➤ Portuguese Sign Language or **Língua Gestual Portuguesa** (LGP) has been developed in 1823 and is the mother tongues of around 10% of the deaf. The official duty of promoting it was set out in the Portuguese Constitution in 1997.

➤ You can find Latin in inscriptions on older monuments and in tribunal façades in the phrase **Domvs Ivstitiae**, i.e. House of Justice.

Kabuverdianu

Let's have a glimpse at Capeverdean Creole, a language based on Portuguese words, but with a different spelling and a very different grammar. It has recently become a co-official language in Cape Verde, along with Portuguese.

Tenba un ómi la Sobradóna. Na stráda sa ta pása un káru ku un munti lus. E' pidi káru pa e' leba-l. Kántu káru pára, kel ómi fla así:

- Ómi, nhu da-m un bulea ti kása-l Batádja!

E' rusponde-l pa e' bai ten ku sinhor katxór la di pa trás. Kel ómi ki pidi bulea, bai fála ku sinhor katxór, sinhor katxór fla-l pa e´subi. Es ben ti kása Batádja, ómi pipa pa e´po-l na txon go. Káru nega pára y, sima e' sa ta pasába pontu, e´grita:

- Krédu!... Avé Mariâ!

Dipos, kántu ki e' fla "Krédu!... Avé Mariâ!", e´xinti ma e´staba na mésmu káu, pundi ki e´pidiba bulea.

T.V. da Silva (2004)
In *Na Bóka Noti, vul.1, 2.º* id. Praia: IBNL. p. 241

There was a man at a place called Sobradona. Along the road came a car with many lights. He asked for the car to take him along. When the car stopped, he said:

- "Sir, give me a ride to Batalha´s house!"

The man answered him to go to Mister Dog who was in the back. The man who had asked for a ride went to speak to Mister Dog. Mister Dog told him to get in the car. When they reached Batalha's house, the man asked loudly to be left there. As the car did not stop and they were already passing the bridge , he shouted:

- Jesus! Hail Mary!

As soon as he said, 'Jesus! Hail Mary!', he found that he was in the same place where he had asked for the ride.

Not only are there many people speaking Capeverdean in Portugal, but Capeverdean music is also very popular. The balad *Sodade* (by Armando Zeferino Soares) in Capeverdean Creole, is familiar to most Portuguese. The origin of the word *saudade*, the Portuguese equivalent of *sodade*, is the old *soledade*, meaning solitude or loneliness, today *solidão*.

Sodade

PORTUGUESE ATTITUDES TOWARDS LANGUAGES

A minha pátria é a língua portuguesa.
My motherland is the Portuguese language.

Fernando Pessoa (1888–1935)
alias Bernardo Soares in *The Book of Disquiet*

"Some years ago the Portuguese authorities started promoting *lusofonia*, a concept based on the idea that language is a motherland or a national flag. Colonialism, expelled through the door of History, is back through the window of language."

Antonio Tabucchi (*Le Monde*, Paris, March 2000)

"I have often said that after the end of the Portuguese empire, the frustrated imperial mission was rebalanced by the transfer to language. This is not particularly bright nor is it seen as particularly bad by the world; a world that actually does not care much about it. [...] It is fundamental for us that the Portuguese language keeps its official status both in the European Union and in the Portuguese-speaking African countries and Timor. [...] Portugal must have strong language policy guidelines, not because of an imperial mission or neo-colonialism but to deepen an historical, undeniable, wanted, and structural fact of the current reality of those countries. Without it, they cannot normalize, modernize, or develop themselves. [...] Furthermore, none of the native languages is able to guarantee such results. [...] Brazil must obviously be seen differently. We are a small country without many resources to compete with English and Spanish besides a potential planetary network of contacts."

Vasco Graça Moura
(*Expresso*, Lisboa, March 2000)

"Language is not a substitute for the lost empire. Nor is *lusofonia* an empire the other way around or a sort of the spiritual Fifth Empire announced by Vieira. The best about the Portuguese language is that it is travel and miscegenation. River of many rivers. And perhaps motherland of several motherlands. There is also the Portuguese language of oppression and of liberation. The one of long and multiple tyrannies and also of several resistances. In Portuguese Brazil declared independence. And Angola, Mozambique, Guinea, Cape Verde, and São Tomé and Príncipe started their liberation. It is the same language. But it is not the same language. It is one. But it is several. The more diverse, the more she is. The more pure, the more impure. The more rich, the more mixed. […] Our language is a language of good prose and good poetry. But not a language of economy or technologies nor of the supremacy of mass media, technocracy and technology. With English, we will not guarantee the cultural personality of our peoples. To renounce language is to renounce soul."

Manuel Alegre
(*Expresso*, Lisboa, March 2000)

Quinto Império

The Portuguese myth of the **Fifth Empire** is inspired by prophet Daniel's biblical visions announcing an eternal empire after four bygone empires. Padre António Vieira (1608–1697) first identified the empire as Portugal's Catholic spiritual mission in Brazil and the world. Then Fernando Pessoa (1888–1935) proclaimed the Fifth Empire to be a Portuguese world empire of culture based on a universal language especially apt for communication, dialogue, poetry, and erudition.

Standard spelling

Between 1911 and 2010 there were several amendments to official spelling, always trying to keep pace with changes in Portugal and in Brazil. That is why spelling has been an issue for more than a hundred years.

Old spelling		Current speling
belleza	⟹	beleza
directo	⟹	direto
grammatica	⟹	gramática
hontem	⟹	ontem
pharmacia	⟹	farmácia
portuguez	⟹	português
prompto	⟹	pronto
sciencia	⟹	ciência
signaes	⟹	sinais
thermometro	⟹	termómetro

Foreign languages

The most widespread foreign languages among the Portuguese, and the only ones taught at school, are English (40%), French (30%), Spanish (10%), and German (5%). Other foreign languages, scarcely taught at university and private language schools, are Dutch, Italian, Russian, and Mandarin. In spite of having a high rate of monolinguals among EU countries, Portugal also has a high rate of people speaking more than two foreign languages.

Romani

The Romani first arrived to Portugal around 1500 and soon became to be persecuted by law and to be called *ciganos* (from Greek *athígganos*, meaning untouchables). Currently, around 0.5% of the population identifies as Romani, and they no longer speak their ancestral Romanó-kaló but a variety of European Portuguese with words of Romani origin.

 **CPLP**
Comunidade dos Países de Língua Portuguesa

Organization of nine countries with Portuguese as their official language

 INSTITUTO INTERNACIONAL DA LÍNGUA PORTUGUESA
IILP

International institute for the Portuguese language

 CAMÕES
INSTITUTO DA COOPERAÇÃO E DA LÍNGUA
PORTUGAL
MINISTÉRIO DOS NEGÓCIOS ESTRANGEIROS

Portuguese institute for the promotion of the Portuguese language abroad

Portugal

Cabo Verde

Guiné-Bissau

Brasil

São Tomé e Príncipe

Lusofonia

Roughly ten years after the independence of all five African colonies, the word **lusofonia** emerged in Portugal to refer either to the whole of those who speak the language around the world or the group of countries that have Portuguese as their official language. Currently, there are nine: Angola, Brazil, Cape Verde, East Timor, Equatorial Guinea, Guinea-Bissau, Mozambique, Portugal and São Tomé and Príncipe, as well as Macau, a special administrative region of China. The word and its meaning are inspired by the French word Francophonie. "Luso" comes from Lusitania, one of the ancient nations of Portugal.

é Equatorial

Timor-Leste

Angola

Moçambique

Tools

3

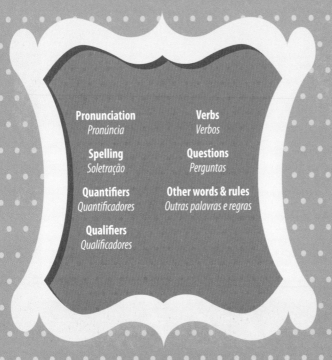

Pronunciation
Pronúncia

Verbs
Verbos

Spelling
Soletração

Questions
Perguntas

Quantifiers
Quantificadores

Other words & rules
Outras palavras e regras

Qualifiers
Qualificadores

Letter(s)	English closest equivalent	Example	Meaning
a, â, à	fat	amanhã	tomorrow
a	about	amanhã	tomorrow
ã, am-, an	ample	amanhã	tomorrow
ão, -am	pound	pão	bread
ãe	saint	mãe	mother
b	banana	banana	banana
c	car	carro	car
ç	sun	caça	hunting
ch	sugar	chá	tea
d	dragon	dragão	dragon
e, é	cheque	ela	she
e, ê	encounter	ele	he
em-, en-	empower	entrada	entrance
-em, -en	saint	tem	(he/she/it) has
e	bake	ele	he
e	feet	real	real
f	favour	favor	favour

Letter(s)	English closest equivalent	Example	Meaning
g	garage	garagem	garage
g	measure	garagem	garage
h	-	hora	hour
i	feet	infinito	infinite
im-, in-	finger	infinito	infinite
j	measure	ginja	black cherry
l	lake	lago	lake
lh	million	milhão	million
m	monkey	macaco	monkey
n	never	nunca	never
nh	onion	vinho	wine
o, ó	lozenge	cobra	cobra
o, ô	book	porto	port
o	loot	porto	port
om-, on-	contrary	contrário	contrary
-õe	boing	põe	(he/she/it) puts
p	person	pessoa	person

Letter(s)	English closest equivalent	Example	Meaning
q	quiet	quieto	quiet
r	preterite	caro	expensive
-r, rr	robbie (Scott.)	carro	car
s	sun	sol	sun
s	easy	casa	house
s	sugar	estrada	road
s	measure	Lisboa	Lisbon
t	taxi	táxi	taxi
u	loot	uva	grape
um-, un-	tomb	um	one
v	vase	vaso	vase
x	sugar	xaile	shawl
x	easy	exame	exam
x	taxi	táxi	taxi
x	sun	máximo	maximum
z	easy	zebra	zebra
z	sugar	luz	light

SPELLING

A a A
águia
á

F f F
faca
éfe

K k K
karaté
capa

P p P
pato
pê

V v V
vaca
vê

B b B
burro
bê

G g G
gato
guê

L l L
laranja
éle

Q q Q
queijo
quê

W w W
windsurf
dâblio

C c C
cão
cê

H h H
hipopótamo
agá

M m M
morango
éme

R r R
rato
érre

X x X
xilofone
xis

D d D
dado
dê

I i I
igreja
i

N n N
nariz
éne

S s S
sapato
ésse

Y y Y
yoga
ípsilon

E e E
elefante
é

J j J
jardim
jota

O o O
olho
ó

T t T
táxi
tê

U u U
uvas
u

Z z Z
zebra
zê

QUANTIFIERS

bocado – bit
metade – half
nada – nothing
número – number
parte – part, portion

0	zero	10	dez		
1	um	11	onze			100	cem (cento)

0	zero	10	dez				
1	um	11	onze			100	cem (cento)
2	dois	12	doze	20	vinte	200	duzentos
3	três	13	treze	30	trinta	300	trezentos
4	quatro	14	catorze	40	quarenta	400	quatrocentos
5	cinco	15	quinze	50	cinquenta	500	quinhentos
6	seis	16	dezasseis	60	sessenta	600	seiscentos
7	sete	17	dezassete	70	setenta	700	setecentos
8	oito	18	dezoito	80	oitenta	800	oitocentos
9	nove	19	dezanove	90	noventa	900	novecentos

21	vinte e um	32	trinta e dois
121	cento e vinte e um	232	duzentos e trinta e dois
1121	mil cento e vinte e um	2232	dois mil duzentos e trinta e dois

QUALIFIERS

Like other words in Portuguese, regular qualifiers have 4 different forms:

-o	masc. sing.	giro, novo, fino	-os	masc. pl.	giros, novos, finos
-a	fem. sing.	gira, nova, fina	-as	fem. pl.	giras, novas, finas

FEIO / UGLY

GIRO / CUTE

GORDO / FAT

MAGRO / SLIM

GRANDE / BIG

PEQUENO / SMALL

PRIMEIRO / FIRST

ÚLTIMO / LAST

LENTO / SLOW

POUCO / FEW

MUITO / MUCH

RÁPIDO / FAST

MELHOR / BETTER

PIOR / WORSE

NOVO / YOUNG

VELHO / OLD

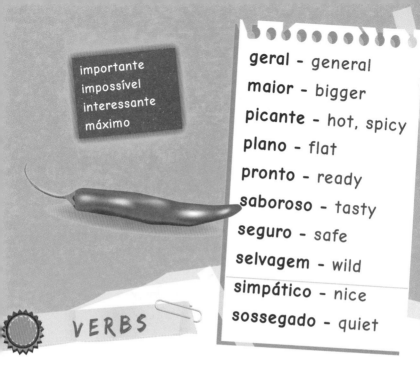

importante
impossível
interessante
máximo

geral - general
maior - bigger
picante - hot, spicy
plano - flat
pronto - ready
saboroso - tasty
seguro - safe
selvagem - wild
simpático - nice
sossegado - quiet

VERBS

Most verbs have 66 different forms. Two of the conditions that make verbs take a certain form, like in English, are person and tense, only in Portuguese these interfere with each other much more. To make it basic, let us concentrate on just **9 forms**, starting with the 3 categories of regular verbs according to their ending in the infinitive form.

Most **regular verbs** and all recently created verbs, like *alunar* (to land on the moon) or *globalizar* (to globalize), belong to the −AR category (*cantar*, to sing). Other regular **categories** end on −ER (*vender*, to sell) and −IR (*partir*, to leave).

PUXAR
TO PULL

EMPURRAR
TO PUSH

CANTAR

INDICATIVO

	PRESENTE	PRETÉRITO IMPERFEITO	PRETÉRITO PERFEITO
eu	canto	cantava	cantei
tu	cantas	cantavas	cantaste
ele/ela/você	canta	cantava	cantou
nós	cantamos	cantávamos	cantámos
vós	cantais	cantáveis	cantastes
eles/elas/vocês	cantam	cantavam	cantaram

	PRETÉRITO-MAIS--QUE-PERFEITO	FUTURO
eu	cantara	cantarei
tu	cantaras	cantarás
ele/ela/você	cantara	cantará
nós	cantáramos	cantaremos
vós	cantáreis	cantareis
eles/elas/vocês	cantaram	cantarão

CONJUNTIVO

	PRESENTE	PRETÉRITO IMPERFEITO	FUTURO
eu	cante	cantasse	cantar
tu	cantes	cantasses	cantares
ele/ela/você	cante	cantasse	cantar
nós	cantemos	cantássemos	cantarmos
vós	canteis	cantásseis	cantardes
eles/elas/vocês	cantem	cantassem	cantarem

	IMPERATIVO	CONDICIONAL	INFINITIVO PESSOAL
eu	—	cantaria	cantar
tu	canta	cantarias	cantares
ele/ela/você	cante	cantaria	cantar
nós	cantemos	cantaríamos	cantarmos
vós	cantai	cantaríeis	cantardes
eles/elas/vocês	cantem	cantariam	cantarem

Though there is a set of forms for the **future**, the Portuguese hardly ever use them when speaking. Instead they use the present forms along with a time clause such as *depois* (after), *amanhã* (tomorrow) or *no futuro* (in the future), somewhat equivalent to English *will* or *shall*. So we will focus on some simple **present** and simple **past** forms.

Each set of forms has 6 forms according to **person**. Here we will skip 2 of them: *tu* (you-singular-informal) which can be replaced with *você* (you--singular-formal), and *vós* (you-plural) which has become regional or an obsolete word and is usually replaced with *vocês* (you-plural). When you use *você* or *vocês*, both being second person, you must use the verb form for the third person, corresponding either to *ele*, *ela* (he, she, it) or *eles*, *elas* (they). Last, we will also show you the verbs forms for the first person *eu* (I) and *nós* (we). As verbs provide inforrmation about the person, one does not often need to use personal pronouns.

TO SING

CANTAR	PRESENT	PAST
eu	canto	cantei
ele/ela/você	canta	cantou
nós	cantamos	cantámos
eles/elas/vocês	cantam	cantaram

TO SELL

VENDER	PRESENT	PAST
eu	vendo	vendi
ele/ela/você	vende	vendeu
nós	vendemos	vendemos
eles/elas/vocês	vendem	venderam

TO LEAVE

PARTIR	PRESENT	PAST
eu	part**o**	part**i**
ele/ela/você	part**e**	part**iu**
nós	part**imos**	part**imos**
eles/elas/vocês	part**em**	part**iram**

Unfortunately, there are too many **irregular verbs**, and they are among the most commonly used. Let us focus on 13 of them, beginning with 3 of the 4 main auxiliary verbs. We will skip **haver**, equivalent to the English **to have**, and with the same origin, because it is a far too irregular a verb, not only in terms of its forms, but especially how it is used. Typically, you can replace it with **ter**, another equivalent of the English **to have**.

The English verb **to be** also has two equivalents in Portuguese. They are the verbs **ser** and **estar**. A simplified way to tell the difference is as follows:

She is a woman. to be (more permanent) **SER** Ela **é** uma mulher.
She is here. to be (less permanent) **ESTAR** Ela **está** aqui.

SER TO BE		
sou	**eu**	fui
é	**ele**	foi
somos	**nós**	fomos
são	**eles**	foram

ESTAR TO BE		
estou	**eu**	estive
está	**ele**	esteve
estamos	**nós**	estivemos
estão	**eles**	estiveram

(Eu) sou uma mulher.   (Eu) estive aqui.

Você é uma mulher.   Você esteve aqui.

(Nós) somos mulheres. (Nós) estivemos aqui.

Elas são mulheres.   Elas estiveram aqui.

In colloquial speech, verb **ESTAR** and all its forms drop the initial ES-. So you will probably hear *'tar* for *estar*; *'tou*, for *estou*; *'tivemos* for *estivemos* and so on. Past forms, like the last one, will sound like verb **TER**.

DAR to give

dou	dei
dá	deu
damos	demos
dão	deram

💡 Nós damos as flores.

We give the flowers.

💡 Eu dei as flores.

I gave the flowers.

DIZER to say

digo	disse
diz	disse
dizemos	dissemos
dizem	disseram

💡 Eles dizem a verdade.

They tell the truth.

💡 Ela disse a verdade.

She told the truth.

FAZER to do

faço	fiz
faz	fez
fazemos	fizemos
fazem	fizeram

💡 Vocês fazem tudo.

You do everything.

💡 Ele fez tudo.

He did everything.

Ir to go

vou	fui
vai	foi
vamos	fomos
vão	foram

💡 Eu vou ao museu.
I go to the museum.

💡 Eles foram ao museu.
They went to the museum.

PODER can

posso	pude
pode	pôde
podemos	pudemos
podem	puderam

💡 Ele pode fazer isso.
He can do it.

💡 Eles puderam fazer isso.
They could do it.

QUERER to want

quero	quis
quer	quis
queremos	quisemos
querem	quiseram

💡 Eles querem comer.
They want to eat.

💡 Você quis comer.
You wanted to eat.

SABER to know

sei	soube
sabe	soube
sabemos	soubemos
sabem	souberam

💡 Você sabe a resposta.
You know the answer.

💡 Nós soubemos a resposta.
We knew the answer.

SAIR to go out

saio	saí
sai	saiu
saímos	saímos
saem	saíram

💡 Eles saem da loja.
They leave the shop.

💡 Ela saiu da loja.
She left the shop.

TER to have

tenho	tive
tem	teve
temos	tivemos
têm	tiveram

💡 Ela tem um carro.
She has a car.

💡 Nós tivemos um carro.
We had a car.

VER to see

vejo	vi
vê	viu
vemos	vimos
veem	viram

💡 Eu vejo uma estrela.
I see a star.

💡 Vocês viram uma estrela.
You saw a star.

VIR to come

venho	vim
vem	veio
vimos	viemos
vêm	vieram

💡 Você vem de Lisboa.
You come from Lisbon.

💡 Elas vieram de Lisboa.
They came from Lisbon.

BACK TO SCARY BASICS

If you find it all too complicated, you can make yourself understood by using only the **infinitive** form along with words that replace the information about **person** and **tense** that other forms contain. But remember to always put the words in the right order: TENSE + PERSON + INFINITIVE.

PAST

Estivemos	Ontem nós estar	Fui	Ontem eu ir
(We were)	Antes nós estar	(I went)	Antes eu ir

PRESENT

Saio	Hoje eu sair	Você vai	Hoje você ir
(I go out)	Agora eu sair	(You go)	Agora você ir

FUTURE

Eles virão	Amanhã eles vir	Ela irá	Amanhã ela ir
(They will come)	Depois eles vir	(She will go)	Depois ela ir

ontem, hoje, amanhã
yesterday, today, tomorrow

antes, agora, depois
before, now, after

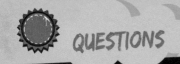

What	O que	O que é isto?	What is this?
	O quê	O quê?!	What?!
Why	Porque	Porque é que não veio?	Why didn't you come?
	Porquê	Mas porquê?	But why?
Which	Qual (sing.)	Qual é o caminho?	Which way is it?
	Quais (pl.)	Quais casas?	Which houses?
Where	Onde	Onde fica o museu?	Where is the museum?
Who	Quem	Quem é ele?	Who is he?
How	Como	Como está?	How are you?
How much	Quanto	Quanto custa?	How much does it cost?
How many	Quantos	Quantos são?	How many are they?

THE PORTUGUESE NEVER SAY YES?

It is true, the Portuguese hardly ever say the word yes. Not because they always say no. Instead of using the word *sim* they use the first verb of the question.

Vai à praia?
Are you going to the beach?

Vou.
Yes, I am.

É bonito?
Is it beautiful?

É.
Yes, it is.

Ela não tinha dito a verdade?
Had she not told the truth?

Tinha.
Yes, she had.

Pagaste à entrada?
Did you pay at the entrance?

Paguei.
Yes, I did.

Otherwise you will hear a lot of *pois* (indeed) and *'tá* (short for *está bem*, it is OK). On the contrary, for negative answers, it is much easier: just use *não*, either alone (no) or before the verb (not). And there is always *talvez* (maybe).

Vai?
Are you going?

Não, não vou.
No, I'm not.

OTHER WORDS & RULES

-ly = -mente
completamente, essencialmente, finalmente, permanentemente, realmente, totalmente

-ary = -ário
contrário, dicionário, extraordinário, monetário, primário, revolucionário

-ty = -dade
cidade, liberdade, qualidade, quantidade, realidade, sociedade

-tion = -ção
ação, competição, intenção, opção, participação, revolução

MAKING WORDS

MAR

amarar - "to land" on water
beira-mar - seaside
maré - tide
maremoto - tsunami
maresia - sea smell
marinha - navy

marinheiro - sailor
marisco - seafood
marítimo - maritime
marulhar - sea sound
submarino - submarine

CRAZY ABOUT ARTICLES

There are only a few circumstances in which you do not need to put an article before a noun. Articles, like their postponed nouns, have 4 forms: masculine or feminine and singular or plural. Let us see the case of the definite article equivalent to **the**: o (masc. sing.), a (fem. sing.), os (masc. pl.), as (fem. pl.):

o carro, a casa, os carros, as casas
the car, the house, the cars, the houses

Sometimes the definite article is attached to a preposition before the noun:

no carro, da casa, aos carros, pelas casas
in the car, of the house, to the cars, by the houses

Before a person's first name you should also put the definite article:

o Pedro, a Maria, a Isabel, o António

Even some places have an article before:

o Porto (Oporto), o Algarve (the Algarve)

PREPOSITIONS & CONECTORS

These two categories of words are among the trickiest to use either because they hardly ever have an exact equivalent in English or because they require a language skill this book will not provide you with. So we will just list a few of them. However, it may be helpful to know e (and) and ou (or).

Preposições   *a, até, com, de, desde, em, entre, para, por, sem*

Conjunções   *como, e, enquanto, mas, ou, portanto, porque, que, se*

POSSESSIVES

There are 6 of them with 4 different forms each.
Just remember *meu* (my) and *seu* (your, his, her, their).

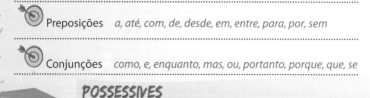

People

4

PEOPLE

BEBÉ
BABY

CRIANÇA
CHILD

HOMEM
MAN

LOIRO
BLOND

MORENO
BRUNETTE

MULHER
WOMAN

RAPARIGA
GIRL

RAPAZ
BOY

gajo	bloke
gente	people
jovem	teenager
pessoa	person

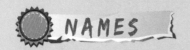

NAMES

Como se chama?

What's your name?

Chamo-me...

My name is...

Qual é o seu primeiro nome?

What's your first name?

Qual é o seu apelido?

What's your family name?

Qual é a sua idade?

How old are you? (formal)

Quantos anos tens?

How old are you? (informal)

AREN'T ALL WOMEN CALLED MARIA?

It is true that most women born before 1974 are called Maria though they would hardly ever use this. In fact, these women's first name is usually a compound of Maria with another name, before or after it. So you can have either Ana Maria or Maria Ana, both addressed to as Ana. A very few are named 'simplesmente' Maria and addressed as Maria. Even men can have Maria in their name, but it is always in the second position. So a woman may be called Maria José, but José Maria is always a man.

POPULAR FIRST NAMES

Ana	Maria	João	José
Joana	Ana	Tiago	António
Sara	Isabel	André	João
Andreia	Anabela	Pedro	Luís
Cátia	Teresa	Ricardo	Carlos
Inês	Helena	Diogo	Pedro
Catarina	Cristina	Fábio	Paulo
Cláudia	Elisabete	Nuno	Fernando
Vanessa	Fernanda	Bruno	Manuel

MALE NICKNAMES

Zé	(José)
Zeca	(José Carlos)
Camané	(Carlos Manuel)
Tomané	(António Manuel)
Tozé	(António José)
Zetó	(José António)
Tó	(António)

CURIO: ZÉ AND MARIA ARE YOUR 'ORDINARY PORTUGUESE'.

DO PEOPLE CREATE NEW NAMES FOR THEIR CHILDREN?

No. That is officially impossible. The law for naming people is very strict and it has been like that since Inquisition times, back in the 16th century. The general law has long established that all first names be Christian names. Later, names of historical heroes were accepted, then foreign names translated or adapted to Portuguese spelling. There are some exceptions, but for the majority of the population, names are supposed to be chosen from a closed pre-established list.

ADDRESS

estrangeiro – foreign, foreigner

solteiro – single

viúvo – widow, widower

POPULATION

Braga

Porto

Coimbra

Ponta Delgada

Lisboa

Évora

Funchal

Faro

Dense population Sparse population

PAÍS DE DOUTORES

Everyone with a degree is supposed to be addressed using *doutor* or *doutora* before their name, whether it is a degree in Medicine, Sociology or Education. Also, people of status but without a degree are often addressed this way. (Some) Portuguese joke about it calling Portugal the '**country of doctors**'. The rest of the men are plainly *senhor*, while women are mostly *dona*. The masculine *dom* is now restricted to high Catholic clergy and past royalty. Written abbreviations are *DR.*, *DRA.*, *SR.* and *SRA.*

Bom dia.	Boa tarde.	Boa noite.
Good morning.	Good afternoon.	Good night.
	Good evening. (before sunset)	Good evening. (after sunset)

Prazer em conhecê-lo/la.	Como está?	Tudo bem?	Olá!
Pleased to meet you.	How do you do?	How are you?	Hello!

Igualmente.	Bem, obrigado.	Tudo bem.	Fixe.	'Tá-se/Tasse?.
Likewise.	Well, thank you.	I'm good.	Cool.	Cool.

Nós vamo-nos embora.	Vamos embora!	Bora!
We are leaving now.	Let's go!	Let's!

Adeus!	Tchau!	Até logo!	Até amanhã!
Goodbye!	Bye!	See you later!	See you tomorrow!

CURIO: On the phone
Calling: (Es)tá lá? (Es)tá?
Answering: (Es)tou! (Es)tá!

Se faz favor.
Please.

sff/s.f.f.
Please. (written abbreviation)

sashavor
Please. (oral abbreviation)

Desculpe.
Sorry.

Com licença.
Excuse me.

'Cença.
Excuse me. (oral abbreviation)

Com certeza.
Of course.

Obrigado. (masc.)
Obrigada. (fem.)
Thank you.

SOME SLANG

 SOFT SLANG

CARAÇAS (HECK)
FOGO (HELL)
MERDA (SHIT)

 HARD SLANG
(never to say, just to understand!)

CARALHO (COCK)
FODA-SE (FUCK IT)
PORRA (DAMN)

HAXE (HASHISH)
ERVA (WEED)
CHARRO (JOINT)
DESBUNDAR (TO REVEL)
DESENRASCANÇO (RESOURCEFULNESS)

"-INHO" OF COURTESY

Portuguese very often use the diminutive suffix *-inho* as a way to show affection to an object or the person they are addressing, among many other uses besides meaning "small". Asking for a *copinho de água* does not mean you want a small glass of water, but rather that you are being nice, informal but kind, to the person you are asking it to. So you will hear *Zezinho* (Joseph), *mãezinha* (mother), *batatinha* (potato), *bananinha* (banana), *chazinho* (tea), *cafezinho* (coffee), *vinhinho* (wine), *garrafinha* (bottle), *pãozinho* (bread), *bacalhauzinho* (cod), *beijinho* (kiss) and even *obrigadinho* (thanks).

De onde é?
Where do you come from?

De que país é? Qual é o seu país?
Which country are you from?

Sou de...	**Sou...**	**Somos de...**	**Somos...**
I come from...	I am...	We come from...	We are...

Fala...?	**Compreende...?**	**Mais alto.**	**Mais devagar.**
Do you speak...?	Do you understand...?	Louder.	Slower.

Falo...	**Compreendo...**	**Não falo...**	**Não compreendo.**
I speak...	I understand...	I do not speak...	I do not understand.

Línguas

alemão, árabe, checo, dinamarquês, espanhol, finlandês, francês, grego, hindi, húngaro, inglês, italiano, japonês, lituano, malaio, mandarim, polaco, russo, suaíli, sueco, turco, ucraniano, zulo.

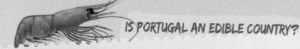

IS PORTUGAL AN EDIBLE COUNTRY?

The country **CAMEROON** is called Camarões in Portuguese, which means shrimps. **PERU** means turkey, the animal, but not TURKEY, the country.

In Turkish, orange is *portakal*, in Greek *portokali* and in Arabic *burtuqal*.

FAMILIES

amigo - friend
casal - couple
namorado - boyfriend
noivo - fiancé
madrinha - godmother
padrinho - godfather
parente/familiar - relative/familiar
vizinho - neighbour

POPULAR FAMILY NAMES

Silva, Santos, Pereira, Ferreira, Costa,
Rodrigues, Martins, Fernandes, Oliveira, Sousa

Some of the most popular family names are taken from plants: *Oliveira* (olive tree), *Pereira* (pear tree) and *Silva* (blackberry bush). *Senhor Silva* is the Portuguese 'ordinary man'.

Other very popular family names are based on male first names, just like Harrison or Johnson in English, and they too used to mean 'child of'. So we have *Rodrigues*, child of Rodrigo, *Martins*, child of Martim, and *Fernandes*, child of Fernando.

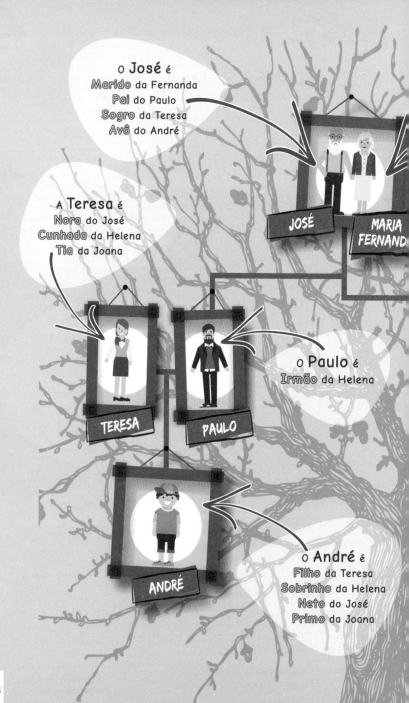

O **José** é
Marido da Fernanda
Pai do Paulo
Sogro da Teresa
Avô do André

A **Teresa** é
Nora do José
Cunhada da Helena
Tia da Joana

O **Paulo** é
Irmão da Helena

O **André** é
Filho da Teresa
Sobrinho da Helena
Neto do José
Primo da Joana

JOSÉ

MARIA
FERNAND

TERESA

PAULO

ANDRÉ

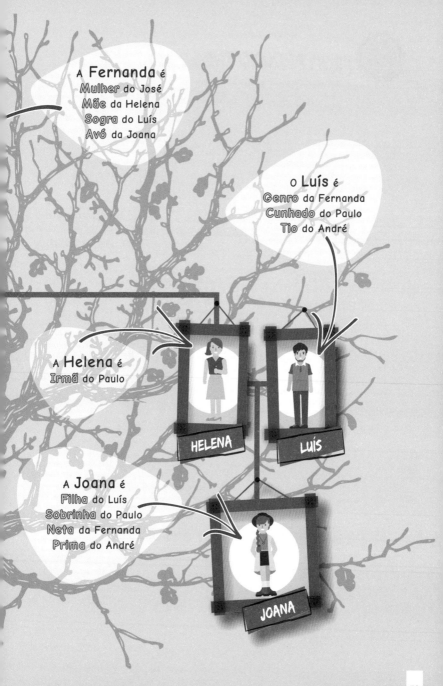

A **Fernanda** é
Mulher do José
Mãe da Helena
Sogra do Luís
Avó da Joana

O **Luís** é
Genro da Fernanda
Cunhado do Paulo
Tio do André

A **Helena** é
Irmã do Paulo

A **Joana** é
Filha do Luís
Sobrinha do Paulo
Neta da Fernanda
Prima do André

HELENA

LUÍS

JOANA

Islândia

Noruega

Canadá

Portugal

Estados Unidos
da América

Marrocos   Ar

México

República
Dominicana

Nicarágua

Senegal

Colômbia   Venezuela

Serra Leo

Guiana

Peru   Brasil

Bolívia

Nam

Chile   Uruguai

Argentina

Finlândia
Lituânia
Rússia
Arménia
Coreia   Japão
Uzbequistão
Jordânia Irão
China
Butão
Paquistão
Arábia Saudita
Tailândia   Filipinas
Índia
e
Camboja
Etiópia
arões
Quénia
Indonésia

mbabué   Madagáscar
Austrália
África do Sul
Nova Zelândia

NACIONALIDADES

australiano, americano, angolano, austríaco,
belga, brasileiro, cabo-verdiano, canadiano,
chinês, guineense, indiano, irlandês,
marroquino, moçambicano, santomense, suíço,
sul-africano, timorense

WHAT IS A TUGA?

Tuga is the inhabitant of 'the garden grown by the sea' or *o jardim à beira-mar plantado* that is Portugal. In Brazil they are called *portuga*. The word *tuga* seems to have originated among African speakers of Portuguese.

PARA INGLÊS VER

'For English to see' > Show-off. This expression seems to have been used first by the crown prince, when the royal family arrived in Brazil, in 1808, fleeing from the French and escorted by the British. The people of Salvador gave them such an enthusiastic welcome that the prince commented that this was a particularly good thing for the English admiral to see.

ΑΒΓΔΕΖΗΘΙΚΛΜΝΞΟΠΡΣΤΥΦΧΨΩ

VER-SE GREGO   *'TO SEE ONESELF GREEK' = TO BE IN TROUBLE*

Popular designation of foreigners

camone	foreigner (from English come on)
gringo	American
brazuca	Brazilian
bife	Brit (from English beef)
franciú	French
nuestros hermanos	Spaniards (our brothers in Spanish)

The Spanish are *nuestros hermanos*, but *de Espanha, nem bom vento, nem bom casamento* or 'from Spain, no good wind, nor good wedding'. The bad *vento suão* is a very hot and dry continental summer wind blowing from the Southeast of Spain. The bad weddings refer to those between Portuguese and Spanish royalty because they threatened independence during different succession crises. Eventually, from 1580 to 1640, bad weddings put the kingdom under Spanish rule.

SHOULD YOU SPEAK SPANISH?

If you can speak Spanish, you will likely make yourself understood anywhere in Portugal. But if you do not want to risk hurting anyone's feelings, make sure people understand that you know you are not speaking their mother tongue. That is not hard! Just start with: *¿Comprende español?* In Portuguese, *Compreende espanhol?*

 **JOBS**

O que faz?
What do you do?

Qual é o seu trabalho?
What's your job?

Sou...
I'm a...

advogado - lawyer
agricultor - farmer
carpinteiro - carpenter
chefe - chief

colega - colleague
comerciante - trader
deputado - member of parliament
dono - owner

eletricista - electrician
emprego - job
empresa - firm
enfermeiro - nurse
escritório - office
médico - doctor
juiz - judge
guia - guide
padre - priest
trabalhador - worker

arquiteto
artista
engenheiro
estudante
jornalista
mecânico
polícia
professor

FEELINGS

Gosta?
Do you like it?

Gosta de...?
Do you like...?

Gosto.
Yes, I do.

Gosto muito.
Yes, I like it a lot.

Adoro!
I love it!

Não, não gosto.
No, I don't like it.

Não gosto muito.
No, I don't like it that much.

Não gosto nada.
No, I don't like it at all.

Acho...
I find it...

Penso que...
I think that...

Parece...
It looks like...

Boa sorte!
Good luck!

abraço - hug
alegria - joy, happiness
amor - love
anedota - joke
beijo - kiss
brincadeira - fun
cansado - tired
chatice - boredom

cheiro - smell
conversa - conversation, talk
desgosto - grief
dúvida - doubt
encontro - meeting
medo - fear
mentira - lie
parvoíce - foolishness
verdade - truth
zangado - angry

companhia
diálogo
diferença
dificuldade

CROSSWORDS

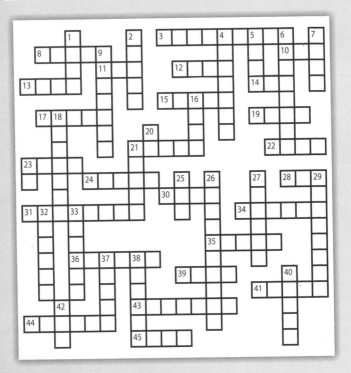

ACROSS

2. guide
4. short for Carlos Manuel
7. to see
8. name
9. mother
11. loud
14. uncle
16. nephew
17. hello
18. American
19. short for António
20. turkey
21. couple
22. people
23. short for José Carlos
25. to be (perm.)
28. American (slang)
29. Brit (slang)
30. to like
32. chief
34. child
37. love
39. neighbour
41. daughter in law

DOWN

1. grandson
2. Greek
3. sister
4. Foreigner (slang)
5. Swedish
6. good
7. wind
10. foreigner
12. cool
13. fun
15. Brazilian (slang)
19. short for Portuguese
20. relative
24. lawyer
26. cool
27. Belgian
31. bye
33. to speak
35. short for António José
36. no, not
38. father
40. short for José

CROSSWORDS

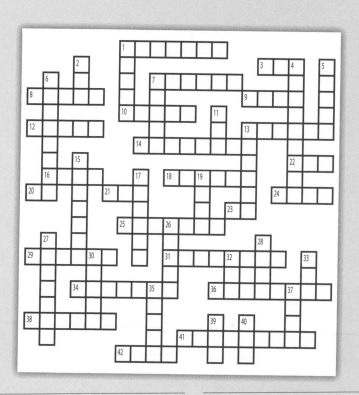

ACROSS		
1.	joke	21. uncle
3.	hello	22. grandfather
7.	short for Carlos Manuel	23. short for António
8.	son in law	24. short for António José
9.	Brit (slang)	25. slow
10.	Russian	29. foreigner (slang)
12.	bye	31. Irish
13.	husband	34. neighbour
14.	olive tree	36. Dutch
16.	parents	38. person
18.	language	41. teacher
20.	short for José	42. sister

DOWN		
1.	to find	27. Japanese
2.	to be (perm.)	28. short for José Carlos
4.	American	30. fiancé
5.	kiss	32. no, not
6.	sorry	33. mother
7.	couple	35. man
11.	father	37. owner
13.	Malay	39. good
15.	dialogue	40. to see
17.	colleague	
19.	daughter in law	
26.	friend	

Getting Around

DIRECTIONS

Qual é o caminho para...?
What is the way to...?

Em que direção fica...?
Which direction is...?

Como vou para...?
How do I get to...?

Sempre em frente.
Straight ahead.

Tem de voltar para trás.
You must turn back.

É complicado.
It's tricky.

A que distância fica...?
How far is it to...?

É longe?
Is it far?

É perto?
Is it near?

Fica a... (minutos/quilómetros)
It's... (min/km) away

É muito longe.
It's very far away.

São só...
It's only...

Fica em frente de...
It's in front of...

Fica ao lado de...
It's next to...

Fica atrás de...
It's behind...

Perigo
Danger

Cuidado!
Be careful!

Atenção!
Pay attention!

MARKING DISTANCE

	Close to speaker	Close to listener	Away from both
Place	aqui (here)	aí (there)	ali (there)
Object	isto (this)	isso (that)	aquilo (that)

SUBIDA DESCIDA ESQUERDA DIREITA ENTRADA SAÍDA DENTRO FORA

AROUND THE COUNTRY

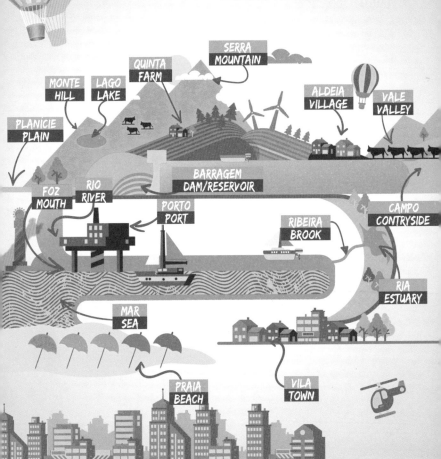

SERRA
MOUNTAIN

QUINTA
FARM

MONTE
HILL

LAGO
LAKE

ALDEIA
VILLAGE

VALE
VALLEY

PLANÍCIE
PLAIN

FOZ
MOUTH

RIO
RIVER

BARRAGEM
DAM/RESERVOIR

PORTO
PORT

RIBEIRA
BROOK

CAMPO
CONTRYSIDE

RIA
ESTUARY

MAR
SEA

PRAIA
BEACH

VILA
TOWN

CIDADE
CITY

NATURAL GEOGRAPHY & TRADITIONAL PROVINCES

Rio Minho

Gerês

Minho

Trás-os-Montes e Alto Douro

Douro Litoral

Marão

Rio Douro

Beira Alta

Rio Mondego

Estrela

Ria de Aveiro

Caramulo

Beira Litoral

Sistema montanhoso Montejunto-Estrela

Beira Baixa

Castelo de Bode

Estremadura

Oeste

Ribatejo

Rio Tejo

Alto Alentejo

Margem Sul

Alqueva

Rio Sado

Rio Guadiana

Baixo Alentejo

Algarve

Serra Algarvia

Ria Formosa

Açores

Madeira

NORTE

OESTE — ESTE / LESTE

SUL

CURRENT REGIONS

Norte

Centro

Região Autónoma dos Açores

Área Metropolitana de Lisboa

Alentejo

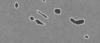

Região Autónoma da Madeira

Algarve

Minho, (river) Minho

Northwestern evergreen hills, birthplace of the country (1143) centred in Braga, former religious head of Galécia or Galiza with archbishop since the 11th century, and Guimarães, seat of the first king.

Mais velho do que a Sé de Braga
Older than Braga's cathedral
(Very old)

Trás-os-Montes, behind the hills

East of Minho, the wide plateau behind a mountain range with 19 peaks over 1000 metres high. It is the remotest part of the country and when people want to name a distant place, the target usually is the small town Freixo de Espada à Cinta.

Beira, border

After 1064, the Southern border of Christian land. It has had several diferent divisions, the most widespread is Beira Litoral (coastal border), Beira Alta (upper border), Beira Baixa (lower border). For several decades before the end of monarchy (1910), the crown prince was the *Príncipe da Beira*, Prince of Beira. Currently the region is also known as Centro (Centre).

Estremadura, extreme (border)

After 1147, the (new) Southern border of Portugal. Currently best known as o Oeste (the West), north of Lisbon, and Península de Setúbal or Margem Sul (Southern bank), south of Lisbon.

Ribatejo, upon Tagus (river)

Mainly the fertile flatland around rio Tejo, also known as lezíria (from Arabic, *al-jazeera*) or Vale do Tejo (Tagus valley).

Alentejo, beyond Tagus (river)

The vast and wide planes south of rio Tejo, with very dry sunny weather, burning in Summer and freezing in Winter. It was once divided into Alto Alentejo (high Alentejo) and Baixo Alentejo (low Alentejo).

Algarve, the West (in Arabic)

From the Arabic phrase *Al-Gharb Al-Andalus* or the West of Iberia (713--1249). During that period, Silves (*Xilb*) was the most flourishing city and the current capital, Faro, owes its name to Hârun, an Islamic ruler.

Madeira, wood

Madeira island is really rich in wood, but not the rest of the archipelago 700 km off the coast of Morocco. Although it had already been occupied, it was first inhabited by the Portuguese, since 1418, the very beginning of the Descobrimentos or 'Discoveries' period. It has been an Autonomous Region since 1976.

Açores, goshawks

There are birds of prey in the nine island archipelago, but no goshawks (*Accipter gentilis*). Some believe it was an error when naming buzzards, some say it was first named by Italian sailors as Azzurre or Blue islands. These volcanic islands halfway between Europe and North America were first inhabited by the Portuguese, since 1431, though legend says it is (one of!) the location of mythical Atlantis. It has been an Autonomous Region since 1976.

NATIONAL PARKS AND UNESCO SITES

Guimarães

Porto

Alto Douro Wine Region

Côa Valley

Batalha Monastery

Coimbra University

Alcobaça Monastery

Convent of Christ

Sintra

Jerónimos and Tower of Belém

Elvas

Évora

Açores

Angra do Heroismo

Pico Wine Region

Madeira

Laurissilva Forest

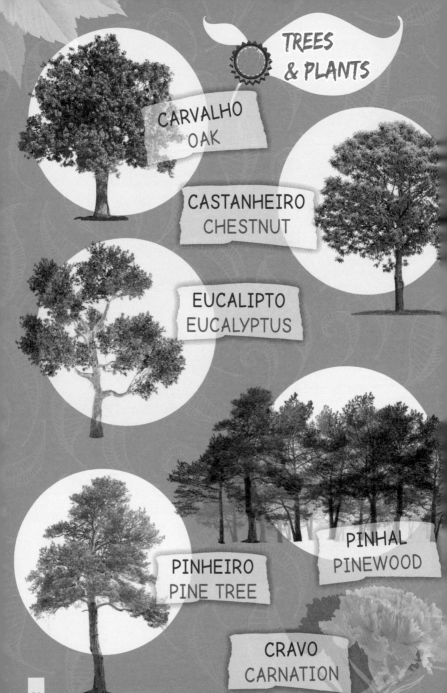

CARVALHO
OAK

CASTANHEIRO
CHESTNUT

EUCALIPTO
EUCALYPTUS

PINHAL
PINEWOOD

PINHEIRO
PINE TREE

CRAVO
CARNATION

OLIVEIRA
OLIVE TREE

PALMEIRA
PALM TREE

SOBREIRO
CORK OAK

ROSA
ROSE

VIDEIRA, VINHA
VINE, VINEYARD

MALMEQUER
DAISY

mal-me-quer bem-me-quer

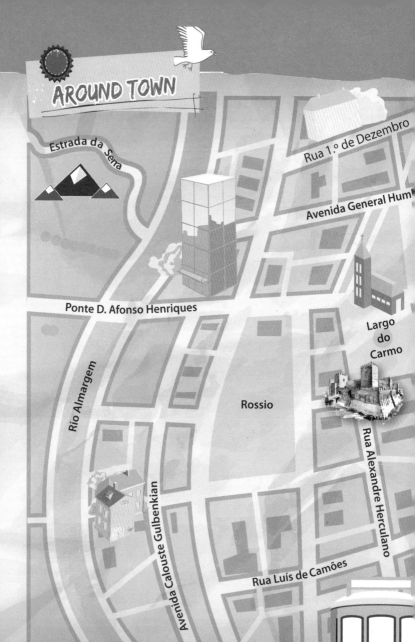

Estrada da Serra

Rua 1.º de Dezembro

Avenida General Hum

Ponte D. Afonso Henriques

Rio Almargem

Largo do Carmo

Rossio

Rua Alexandre Herculano

Avenida Calouste Gulbenkian

Rua Luís de Camões

MAPA

Praça Infante D. Henrique

Rua 5 de Outubro

Rua 31 de Janeiro

Rua Marquês de Pombal

Rua Marquês de Pombal

Parque da Cidade

Avenida da Liberdade

Jardim 25 de Abril

Avenida Francisco Sá Carneiro

Rua Miguel Bombarda

Bairro Combatentes da Grande Guerra

RUA 1º DE DEZEMBRO

1.º de Dezembro, December 1st

The day Portugal restored independence in 1640, after 60 years of Spanish rule. It is a national holiday. Some royalists also celebrate the day of independence (in 1143). Also known as *Restauração* or *Restauradores*.

5 de Outubro, October 5th

This was the day of the proclamation of the Republic, in 1910 (from the balcony of the Lisbon City Hall). Two years before, king D. Carlos I and the crown prince had been shot dead at close range at *Terreiro do Paço*.

31 de Janeiro, January 31st

On this day, a rebellion took place in Oporto in 1891. It was the first movement trying to implement a Republican regime in the country.

25 de Abril, April 25th

The day of the *Revolução dos Cravos* (Carnation Revolution, 1974), the overthrow of the dictatorship lead by mid-rank militia officers who rejected the war in Africa. The revolutionary time, called *PREC - Processo Revolucionário Em Curso* (revolutionary process under way), eventually gave way to democracy in April 1976.

Calouste Gulbenkian (1869-1955)

British philanthropist and millionaire of Armenian origin. In 1956, according to his will, was created the *Fundação Calouste Gulbenkian*, in Lisbon, for decades considered the "ministry" of science and culture.

Alexandre Herculano (1810-1877)

Historian, novelist and poet, one of the introducers of Romanticism, fought for the Liberals in the 1830s. Some of his masterpieces are the novel *Eurico, o Presbítero* and particularly his *História de Portugal*.

Carmo, Carmel

The Roman Catholic *Ordem dos Irmãos de Nossa Senhora do Monte Carmelo* (Order of the Brothers of Our Lady of Mount Carmel) also known as *Carmelitas* (Carmelites) founded in the 12th century. It was later divided into three different orders, one for friars, one for nuns and one for laypeople. Streets with this name usually are next to churches, monasteries or convents of *Carmo*. It is also a popular female first name: *Maria do Carmo*.

Combatentes da Grande Guerra, Combatants of the Great War

Portuguese soldiers during World War I (1914-1918) who fought in Northern France and Belgium, namely in the Battle of La Lys or Ypres (1918). Also just known as *Combatentes*.

D. Afonso Henriques (1109-1185)

The first king of Portugal, son of count D. Henrique, a crusader from the House of Burgundy, and countess Teresa, illegitimate daughter of the king of Castile and Leon. After his father's death, he fought against his mother for the independence of the *Condado Portucalense* in a process that lasted from 1128 to 1179.

Francisco Sá Carneiro (1934-1980)

The first centre-right prime-minister elected after the *Revolução dos Cravos*, who died in a plane crash in Camarate, just off the Lisbon airport, along with the minister of defence during campaign time.

The investigation of the plane crash never lead to consistent conclusions, and the 'Caso Camarate' has become a landmark in national politics and justice affairs.

General Humberto Delgado (1906-1965)

During the *Estado Novo* (New State) dictatorship (1926-1974), Humberto Delgado, *o general sem medo* (the fearless general), was the only candidate for the Portuguese presidency to ever defy Salazar. When, running for President in 1958, he proffered what would become one of the most famous quotes in Portuguese politics, referring to Salazar: *'Obviamente, demito-o!'* (Obviously, I will sack him!). He was killed by the secret police in 1965, near the border in Spain. Naturally, streets received the name of this Airforce officer only after 1974.

Infante D. Henrique, Henry the Navigator (1394-1460)

One of the most famous personalities of Portuguese history, son of king D. João I and the English princess Philippa of Lancaster, founders of the Aviz dynasty. This marriage sealed the Anglo-Portuguese Alliance (1373) still in force today. Infante D. Henrique was governor of the wealthy *Ordem de Cristo*, the Portuguese successor of the Knights Templar, and patron of the first seafarer voyages along the West African coast.

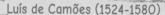

Luís de Camões (1524-1580)

Considered Portugal's greatest poet, author of the epic poem *Os Lusíadas*, 1572 (*The Lusiads*, that is, the Portuguese), about the first voyage between Europe and India, by Vasco da Gama (1498). Camões himself lived in India for nearly twenty years and died in Lisboa in 1580, the same month the Spanish navy sailed into the city giving way to 60 years of foreign rule. For more than a century, Camões has been the ultimate symbol of Portuguese national pride. June 10th represents not only the day he died, but also the Day of Portugal.

Marquês de Pombal, Marquis of Pombal (1699-1782)

The prime minister of king D. José I, rebuilder of Lisboa after the earthquake in 1755. This enlightened authoritarian implemented many political, social, and economic reforms. Education became a matter of State, not of the Church, Portuguese language became compulsory in primary school, instead of Latin, and racial discrimination and death penalty for religious reasons were abolished.

Miguel Bombarda (1851-1910)

Republican and Psychiatrist who fought monarchy, he was murdered two days before the instauration of the Republican regime.

Nuno Álvares Pereira (1360-1431)

Also known as Nun'Álvares or o *Santo Condestável* (the Saint Constable), was the chief commander of the Portuguese army when Portugal, was under threat of annexation in 1383-1385, since the only direct heir to the throne was the Portuguese wife of the Spanish king. Nuno Álvares Pereira's victory at Aljubarrota gave way to the new Aviz dynasty lead by king D. João I. After the death of his wife, Nun'Álvares became a friar at Lisboa's *Convento do Carmo*. He was canonized in 2009.

Rossio

First recorded in 1258, this is general name meaning a large public field or square. Currently, many cities and towns have their Rossio, which most of the times it is the main central square, like in Lisboa. Here, though, Rossio has not been the official name since the 19th century.

BUILDINGS

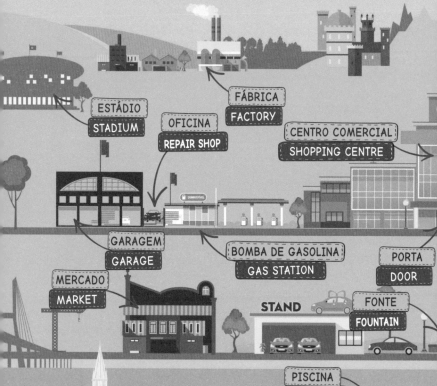

FÁBRICA
FACTORY

ESTÁDIO
STADIUM

OFICINA
REPAIR SHOP

CENTRO COMERCIAL
SHOPPING CENTRE

GARAGEM
GARAGE

BOMBA DE GASOLINA
GAS STATION

PORTA
DOOR

MERCADO
MARKET

STAND

FONTE
FOUNTAIN

PISCINA
SWIMMING POOL

ESTÁTUA
STATUE

MOINHO
WINDMILL

CAPELA
CHAPEL

SÉ / CATEDRAL
CATHEDRAL

ARMAZÉM
STORE

PRÉDIO
BUILDING

IGREJA
CHURCH

RÉS DO CHÃO
GROUNDFLOOR

SUPERMERCADO

CASA
HOUSE

construção
monumento
museu

Vou apanhar o autocarro.
I'm going to catch the bus.

Perdi o comboio.
I missed the train.

Vou de avião.
I'm going by plane.

Gosto de andar de bicicleta.
I like riding a bicycle.

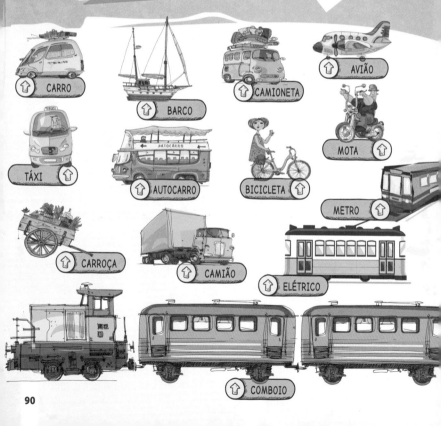

CARRO

BARCO

CAMIONETA

AVIÃO

TÁXI

AUTOCARRO

BICICLETA

MOTA

METRO

CARROÇA

CAMIÃO

ELÉTRICO

COMBOIO

▷ WC
▷ TOILETE
▷ LAVABOS ▷ SANITÁRIOS

TRAVELLING

BILHETEIRA

Onde é a bilheteira?
Where's the ticket office?

Fila única.
Single queue.

Qual é o destino?
What's the destination?

Para onde quer ir?
Where do you want to go to?

Quero dois bilhetes para...
I want two tickets to...

Quero ir para...
I want to go to...

Bilhete de ida e volta?
Return ticket?

Só de ida.
Single only.

Em que classe?
Which class?

Em segunda.
Second class.

Qual é a linha para...?
What's the platform to...?

✈ PARTIDAS

DUBAI 09:50
PRAGA 10:30
⬏ CHEGADAS
PARIS 10:05
LONDRES 11:00

CHEGADAS

JOHN SMITH

escala	stopover
horário	schedule
paragem	stop
seguro	insurance
trânsito	transit
viagem	trip

aeroporto
classe
destino
documento
passaporte
transporte

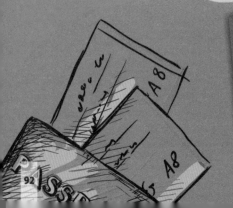

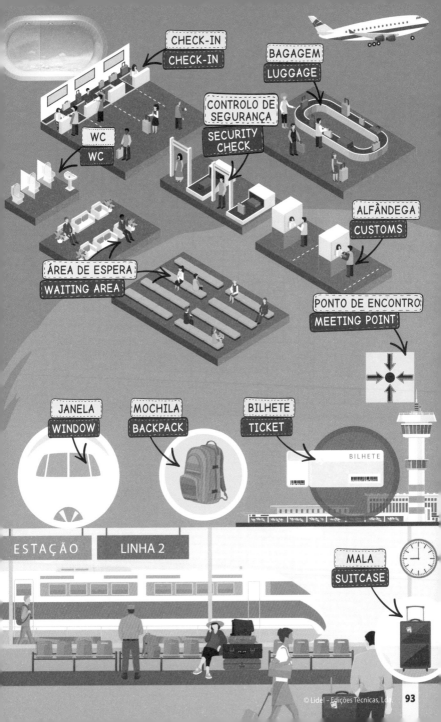

CHECK-IN
CHECK-IN

BAGAGEM
LUGGAGE

CONTROLO DE SEGURANÇA
SECURITY CHECK

WC
WC

ALFÂNDEGA
CUSTOMS

ÁREA DE ESPERA
WAITING AREA

PONTO DE ENCONTRO
MEETING POINT

JANELA
WINDOW

MOCHILA
BACKPACK

BILHETE
TICKET

BILHETE

ESTAÇÃO   LINHA 2

MALA
SUITCASE

CROSSWORDS

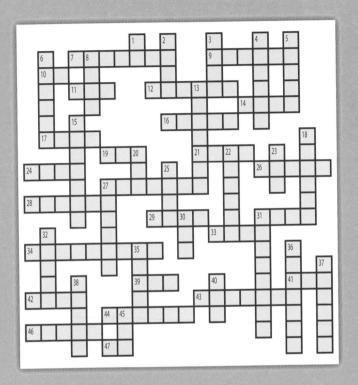

ACROSS

7. castle	28. church
9. spider	29. to
10. to go	31. fear
11. south	33. wolf
12. garden	34. bicycle
14. cat	39. river
16. port	41. sea
17. lion	42. map
19. street	43. factory
21. how	44. bee
24. house	46. donkey
26. fly	47. there (near)
27. care	

DOWN

1. cathedral	25. suitcase
2. rose	27. horse
3. taxi	30. estuary
4. animal	31. mosquito
5. field	32. vineyard
6. pine wood	35. tower
8. here	36. store
13. direction	37. tree
15. garage	38. car
18. monkey	40. dog
20. there (far)	45. ox
22. mill	
23. river mouth	

CROSSWORDS

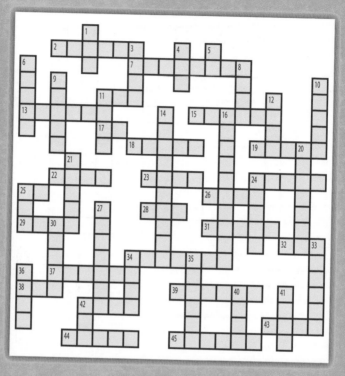

2. travel
7. left
11. dog
13. plant
15. way up
17. cathedral
18. houses
19. way out
22. wolf
23. to
24. mountain
25. there (near)
26. rose
28. river mouth
29. that (near)
31. west
32. ox
34. arrival
37. that (far)
38. south
39. sparrow
42. mouse
43. suitcase
44. goat
45. neighbourhood

1. sea
3. fear
4. street
5. to go
6. field
8. here
9. square
10. snake
11. house
12. map
14. passport
16. library
20. direction
21. wild bull
24. saint
25. there (far)
27. right
30. sign
33. church
34. how
35. spider
36. this
40. goshawk
41. lion
42. estuary

ACROSS

1. mouse
4. country
7. sign
8. west
9. small town
14. to want
16. repair shop
17. there (far)
18. square
19. care
20. dog
21. river
23. to
25. tower
27. motorbike
30. dove
31. cathedral
32. here
34. there (near)
36. museum
39. wood
40. small square
41. cat
42. vineyard
43. oak
44. river mouth
45. map

DOWN

1. street
2. travel
3. sea
5. cork oak
6. pine wood
10. way up
11. way down
12. plane
13. horse
15. rose
17. airport
18. port
19. carnation
22. ox
24. wolf
26. estuary
28. animal
29. old
30. beach
32. attention
33. south
35. neighbourhood
37. way out
38. spider
41. cock

Time & Weather

6

CALENDAR

Em que data?	Em que mês?	Em que dia?
Which date?	Which month?	Which day?

A 16 de julho de 2019.	Em julho.	Na quinta-feira.	No dia 16.
In July 16th 2019.	In July.	On thursday.	On the 16th.

SEMANA
WEEK

ANO
YEAR
2019

MÊS
MONTH

SEGUNDA-FEIRA
(2.º-SEG)

TERÇA-FEIRA
(3.º-TER)

QUARTA-FEIRA
(4.º-QUA)

QUINTA-FEIRA
(5.º-QUI)

SEXTA-FEIRA
(6.º-SEX)

SÁBADO
(S-SAB)

DOMINGO
(D-DOM)

JANEIRO

SEG		7	14	21	28
TER	1	8	15	22	29
QUA	2	9	16	23	30
QUI	3	10	17	24	31
SEX	4	11	18	25	
SAB	5	12	19	26	
DOM	6	13	20	27	

FEVEREIRO

SEG		4	11	18	25
TER		5	12	19	26
QUA		6	13	20	27
QUI		7	14	21	28
SEX	1	8	15	22	
SAB	2	9	16	23	
DOM	3	10	17	24	

MARÇO

SEG		4	11	18	25
TER		5	12	19	26
QUA		6	13	20	27
QUI		7	14	21	28
SEX	1	8	15	22	29
SAB	2	9	16	23	30
DOM	3	10	17	24	31

ABRIL

SEG	1	8	15	22	29
TER	2	9	16	23	30
QUA	3	10	17	24	
QUI	4	11	18	25	
SEX	5	12	19	26	
SAB	6	13	20	27	
DOM	7	14	21	28	

MAIO

SEG		6	13	20	27
TER		7	14	21	28
QUA	1	8	15	22	29
QUI	2	9	16	23	30
SEX	3	10	17	24	31
SAB	4	11	18	25	
DOM	5	12	19	26	

JUNHO

SEG		3	10	17	24
TER		4	11	18	25
QUA		5	12	19	26
QUI		6	13	20	27
SEX		7	14	21	28
SAB	1	8	15	22	29
DOM	2	9	16	23	30

JULHO

SEG	1	8	15	22	29
TER	2	9	16	23	30
QUA	3	10	17	24	31
QUI	4	11	18	25	
SEX	5	12	19	26	
SAB	6	13	20	27	
DOM	7	14	21	28	

AGOSTO

SEG		5	12	19	26
TER		6	13	20	27
QUA		7	14	21	28
QUI	1	8	15	22	29
SEX	2	9	16	23	30
SAB	3	10	17	24	31
DOM	4	11	18	25	

SETEMBRO

SEG		2	9	16	23	30
TER		3	10	17	24	
QUA		4	11	18	25	
QUI		5	12	19	26	
SEX		6	13	20	27	
SAB		7	14	21	28	
DOM	1	8	15	22	29	

OUTUBRO

SEG		7	14	21	28
TER	1	8	15	22	29
QUA	2	9	16	23	30
QUI	3	10	17	24	31
SEX	4	11	18	25	
SAB	5	12	19	26	
DOM	6	13	20	27	

NOVEMBRO

SEG		4	11	18	25
TER		5	12	19	26
QUA		6	13	20	27
QUI		7	14	21	28
SEX	1	8	15	22	29
SAB	2	9	16	23	30
DOM	3	10	17	24	

DEZEMBRO

SEG		2	9	16	23	30
TER		3	10	17	24	31
QUA		4	11	18	25	
QUI		5	12	19	26	
SEX		6	13	20	27	
SAB		7	14	21	28	
DOM	1	8	15	22	29	

FIM DE SEMANA
WEEKEND

DIA
DAY

Days by number

In medieval times, *domingo* (the day of God, Sunday) was market or fair day because people come together to go to church. Thus, the following days became the second fair (*segunda-feira*), the third fair (*terça-feira*) and so on. To abbreviate you can say only the first word and write numbers instead. Thursday, for instance, you can write 5.º or just 5. You can also use the first three letters of each word. Beware, *SEX* in a Portuguese calendar only means *sexta-feira*, Friday!

ZODÍACO

 AQUÁRIO
 PEIXES
 CARNEIRO
 TOURO
 GÉMEOS
 CARANGUEJO

 LEÃO
 VIRGEM
 BALANÇA
 ESCORPIÃO
SAGITÁRIO
CAPRICÓRNIO

TELLING THE TIME

A que horas?	Que horas são?	Quanto tempo falta para...?
At what time?	What time is it?	How long...?

É uma hora.

São duas horas.

São três e um quarto.

São quatro e meia.

São cinco menos um quarto.

03.00	três da manhã	15.00 três da tarde
10.00	dez da manhã	22.00 dez da noite
12.00	meio-dia	24.00 meia-noite

futuro
hora
minuto
momento

amanhã - tomorrow
cedo - early
data - date
feriado - holiday
férias - holidays
hoje - today
horário - timetable
manhã - morning
noite - night, evening
      (after sunset)
nunca - never
ontem - yesterday
relógio - clock, watch
século - century
sempre - always
tarde - afternoon, evening
      (before sunset)
tarde - late

SEASONS

LUA

SOL

INVERNO   PRIMAVERA   VERÃO   OUTONO

WEATHER & ENVIRONMENT

Como está o tempo?
What's the weather like?

Qual é a previsão do tempo para amanhã?
What's the weather forecast for tomorrow?

Está...
It is...

A previsão é...
The forecast is...

ambiente - environment
ar - air
calor - heat
céu - sky
geada - frost
fogo - fire
fresco - cool
frio - cold
lixo - garbage
quente - hot
tempestade - thunder storm
temporal - storm
terra - land, ground

humidade
temperatura

Nortada

From June to September the strong North wind on the west coast blowing from noon to sunset.

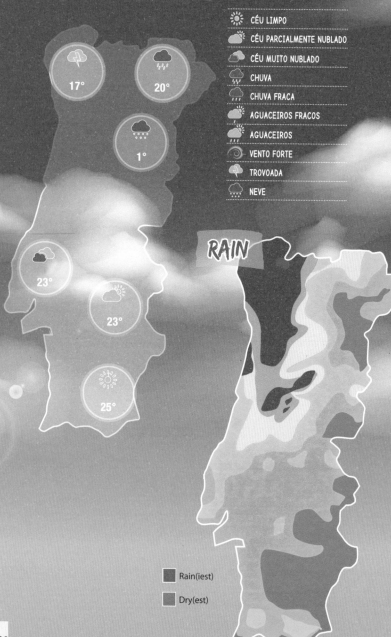

WEATHER FORECAST

Icon	Description
	CÉU LIMPO
	CÉU PARCIALMENTE NUBLADO
	CÉU MUITO NUBLADO
	CHUVA
	CHUVA FRACA
	AGUACEIROS FRACOS
	AGUACEIROS
	VENTO FORTE
	TROVOADA
	NEVE

17°
20°
1°
23°
23°
25°

RAIN

Rain(iest)

Dry(est)

TEMPERATURE JAN

TEMPERATURE JUL

- Cold(est)
- Warm(est)

- Hot(est)
- Cool(est)

 CROSSWORDS

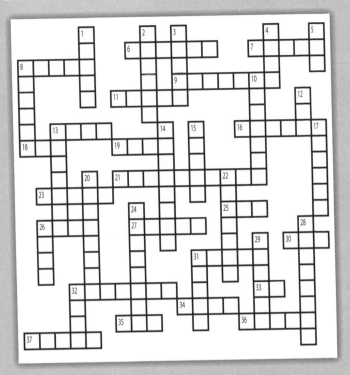

ACROSS

6. future
7. time
8. April
9. timetable
11. wind
13. May
16. holidays
18. year
19. cold
21. calendar
23. yesterday
25. moon
26. today
27. March
30. month
31. evening
32. Sunday
33. air
34. snow
35. sky
36. heat
37. Summer

DOWN

1. July
2. Autumn
3. June
4. early
5. sun
8. tomorrow
10. Winter
12. day
13. moment
14. November
15. frost
17. Saturday
20. December
22. clock
24. environment
26. hour
28. September
29. week
31. cloud
32. date

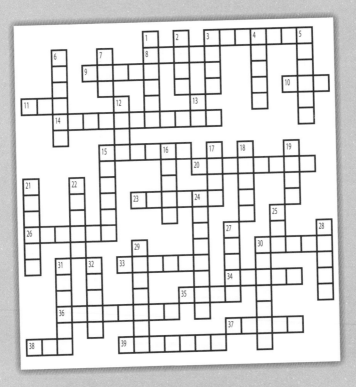

ACROSS

3. timetable
8. March
9. never
10. sun
11. sky
14. temperature
15. week
20. pollution
23. hot
26. Saturday
30. morning
33. future
34. weather
35. May
36. September
37. yesterday
38. year
39. Sunday

DOWN

1. tomorrow
2. cold
3. hour
4. April
5. Autumn
6. minute
7. moon
12. snow
13. air
15. century
16. cloud
17. today
18. July
19. date
21. cool
22. Summer
24. storm
25. day
27. wind
28. late
29. October
30. moment
31. August
32. night

CROSSWORDS

4. January	21. September
6. November	24. early
7. week	26. heat
8. sky	27. never
9. month	28. today
11. time	30. moon
13. cold	31. Saturday
14. storm	34. morning
18. north wind	35. April
19. century	36. tomorrow
20. hour	38. watch

1. cool	22. holidays
2. snow	23. May
3. date	24. rain
5. wind	25. polution
6. cloud	29. Summer
10. sun	32. year
12. March	33. day
13. future	37. air
15. August	
16. yesterday	
17. frost	

2. environment
8. humidity
10. pollution
11. June
15. snow
16. weather
19. Summer
20. hot
21. today
22. September
24. August
27. cold
28. heat
29. moon
31. sky
33. midday
34. air
35. never
36. year
37. timetable

1. storm
2. April
3. night
4. day
5. clock
6. early
7. late
9. minute
11. July
12. Autumn
13. February
14. moment
17. future
18. month
23. sun
24. tomorrow
25. October
26. thunder storm
28. rain
30. century
32. hour
33. May

Food & Drinks

PORTUGUESE ARE THE EUROPEANS THAT EAT MORE

SOPA **ARROZ** **PEIXE**

WHERE

adega - cellar
cozinha - kitchen
cervejaria - beer house
marisqueira - seafood restaurant
mercearia - grocer's
pastelaria - pastry shop
padaria - bakery
taberna - tavern
talho - butcher's

bar
café
litro
restaurante
supermercado

Tenho fome. — I'm hungry.
Tenho sede. — I'm thirsty.

comida - food
bebida - drink
fome - hunger
sede - thurst
gelo - ice

SOFT DRINKS

água - water
chá - tea
leite - milk
sumo - juice

light black coffee
carioca

COFFEE

Coffee	Black	With Milk
Large	café duplo	galão
Medium	bica / cimbalino	meia de leite
Small	italiana	garoto / pingo

WINE

vinho branco - white wine

vinho tinto - red wine

vinho verde - unripe or young wine

Port wine is not a wine of ports, but the wine from Oporto – **vinho do Porto**. Actually, this sweet wine is produced up along the Douro river valley and stored down at Gaia, which lies opposite Oporto. The British have been instrumental in its production and trade since the very beginning (since the end of the 17th century). In 1756 the Marquês de Pombal established the first controlled wine region in History, in the Douro valley.

CONTROLLED WINE REGIONS

Minho

Dão

Douro

Bairrada

Bucelas

Alentejo

Açores

Setúbal

Pico

Madeira

Madeira

Lagoa

BEER & SPIRITS

WHISKY
VODKA
GIN

aguardente - brandy

bagaço - brandy

cerveja - beer

imperial - regular draught beer

fino - regular draught beer (North of Portugal)

caneca - large draught beer

VEGETABLES & CEREALS

- PIMENTO
- COUVE
- BATATA
- FEIJÃO
- ALFACE
- CEBOLA
- ALHO
- SALSA
- CENOURA
- MILHO

Centeio - Rye | Legumes - Vegetables
Trigo - Wheat

popular rice dishes

MAIN DISH: **Arroz de Marisco** (seafood), **Arroz de Tamboril** (monkfish), **Arroz de Pato** (duck); SIDE DISH: **Arroz Branco** (plain), **Arroz de Tomate** (tomato), **Arroz de Grelos** (greens), **Arroz de Feijão** (red bean).

FRUIT & NUTS

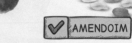
AMENDOIM

AMEIXA

AMÊNDOA

CEREJA

CASTANHA

ANANÁS

LARANJA

FIGO

MELANCIA

MAÇÃ

LIMÃO

MELOA

MORANGO

PÊSSEGO

NOZ

PERA

UVAS

MELÃO

BANANA

fruta - fruit in general
fruto - single fruit

TANGERINA

116

SARDINHA - SARDINE

AMÊIJOA - CLAM

ATUM - TUNA

CAMARÃO - SHRIMP

LAGOSTA - LOBSTER

CARAPAU - HORSE MACKEREL

CARANGUEJO - CRAB

OVAS - SPAWN

LINGUADO - FLOUNDER

SALMÃO - SALMON

LULA - SQUID

PERCEBES - BARNACLES

PEIXE-ESPADA - HAIRTAIL

PESCADA - HAKE

TRUTA - TROUT

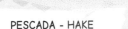

POLVO - OCTOPUS

117

cod

Bacalhau à Brás mixed stir fried shredded cod, fried potatoes, scrambled eggs, onion, parsley, **Bacalhau à Gomes de Sá** mixed boiled shredded cod, boiled potatoes, boiled eggs, onion, black olives, parsley, in the oven, **Bacalhau com natas** mixed boiled shredded cod, potatoes, butter, cream, laurel and clove, in the oven, **Bacalhau à lagareiro** deep fried thick steaks of cod, deep fried potatoes, garlic, in the oven, **Bacalhau com todos** boiled thick steaks of cod, boiled potatoes, boiled eggs, boiled cabbage, **Pastéis de bacalhau** deep fried balls of boiled shredded cod, mashed potato, parsley.

IDIOMS

Pela boca morre o peixe
"By the mouth dies the fish"
Words reveal the speaker's faults

Ficar em águas de bacalhau
"To stay in waters of cod"
To stay unchanged (after trying)

MEAT

CABRITO

PERDIZ

CARNEIRO

COELHO

FRANGO

PATO

PERU

POMBO

PORCO

RÃ

VACA

popular meat dishes

Feijoada stewed beans, pork, sausages, **Cozido à Portuguesa** full variety of boiled meat, sausages, vegetables, **Rojões** stir fried pork, wine, garlic, laurel, **Carne de Porco à Alentejana** stir fried pork, clams, fried potatoes, **Bitoque** small beefsteak, fried potatoes, fried egg, plain rice, salad, **Frango Assado** roasted chicken.

IDIOMS

Dar gato por lebre
"To give cat for hare"
To buy a pig in a poke

Engolir um sapo
"To swallow a toad"
Eventually accept
something unwillingly

Fazer figura de urso
"To make picture of bear"
To act foolish

MEALS

açúcar - sugar
almoço - lunch
assado - roasted
azeite - olive oil
carne - meat
comida - food
cozido - boiled
doce - sweet
farinha - flour
frito - fried
grelhado - grilled
jantar - dinner
lanche - mid-afternoon snack
          or evening tea

manteiga - butter
massa - pasta
papa - mush
pequeno-almoço - breakfast
pimenta - pepper
piripíri - chilli
refeição - meal
sal - salt
sobremesa - dessert
sopa - soup
vinagre - vinegar

popular soups

Caldo-verde cabbage, **Puré de Legumes** vegetables, **Sopa da Pedra** vegetables, red beans, pork strips, **Sopa Alentejana** coriander, bread, egg, garlic, olive oil, **Canja** chicken strips, rice, **Creme de Marisco** seafood, **Sopa de Peixe** fish.

OVO

PÃO

BIFE

QUEIJO

SANDES

BOLO

CHOCOLATE

TORRADA

CACHORRO

SALADA

GELADO

TOSTA

CONTROLLED OLIVE OIL REGIONS

- Trás-os-Montes
- Azeitona
- Beira Interior
- Ribatejo
- Norte Alentejo
- Alentejo Interior
- Moura

CONTROLLED CHEESE REGIONS

- Trás-os-Montes
- Serra da Estrela
- Rabaçal
- Beira Baixa
- Nisa
- Évora
- Azeitão
- Serpa
- Pico
- S. Jorge

SWEET EATERIES

Doçaria Conventual
Convent confectionery with egg yolk and sugar.
Papo de Anjo Angel Crop, Barriga de Freira Nun Belly, Fios de Ovos Egg Threads, Trouxa de Ovos Egg Packs, Ovos Moles Soft Eggs, Lampreia de Ovos Egg Lamprey, Pastel de Nata Egg Tart, Orelha de Abade Abbot Ear, Pingo de Vela Candle Drop, Toucinho do Céu Heavenly Bacon, Pão de Ló Sponge Cake.

Pastelaria
Semi-industrial confection at pastry shops and cafés.
Jesuíta Jesuit: puff pastry, egg cream, preserved fig--leave gourd, cinnamon; Pirâmide Pyramid: trimmings dough, chocolate; Queijada Cottage Cheese Cake; Bola de Berlim Ball of Berlin: fried brioche; Rim Kidney: choux pastry, pastry cream, chocolate; Travesseiro Throw Pillow: puff pastry, egg cream, preserved fig-leave gourd; Guardanapo Napkin: roulade butter cake, egg cream; Bolo de Arroz Rice Cake: butter cake; Caracol Snail: brioche, candied fruit, pastry cream; Queque Butter Cake; Bom-Bocado Good Bit: sweet doug, custard, lemon; Pão de Deus Bread of God: brioche, coconut; Bolo de Coco Coconut Tart: shortcrust, coconut; Pastel de Feijão Bean Tart: shortcrust, white bean, almond.

Sobremesas
Desserts
Arroz-Doce Sweet Rice: rice pudding, Baba de Camelo Camel Dribble: caramel mousse, Pudim Flã Flan pudding, Bolo de Bolacha Biscuit Cake: biscuit, coffee, cream, egg yolk, Leite-Creme Milk Cream Custard, Maçã Assada Roasted Apple, Musse de Chocolate Chocolate Mousse, Doce da Avó Grandmother Dessert: egg yolk, cream, almond, biscuit.

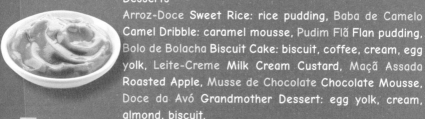

AT THE TABLE

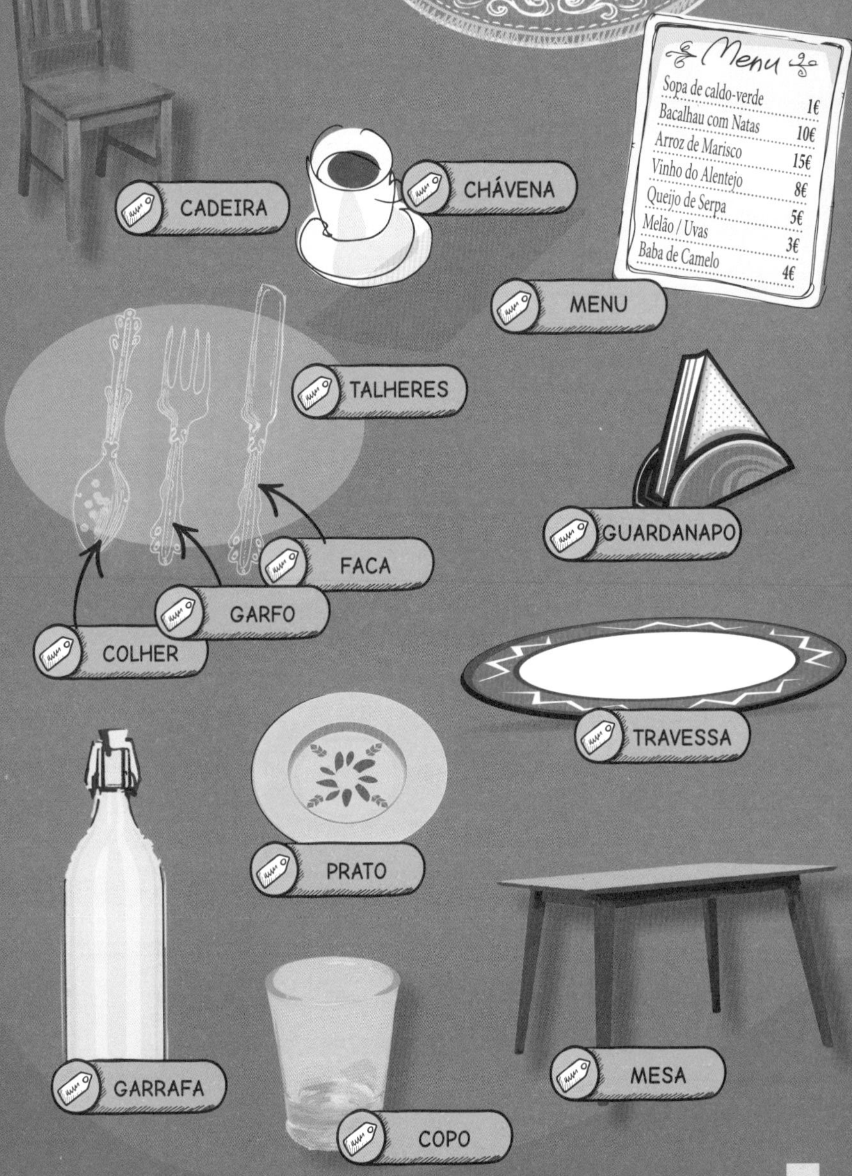
Menu
Sopa de caldo-verde 1€
Bacalhau com Natas 10€
Arroz de Marisco 15€
Vinho do Alentejo 8€
Queijo de Serpa 5€
Melão / Uvas 3€
Baba de Camelo 4€
CADEIRA
CHÁVENA
MENU
TALHERES
GUARDANAPO
FACA
GARFO
COLHER
TRAVESSA
PRATO
GARRAFA
MESA
COPO

CROSSWORDS

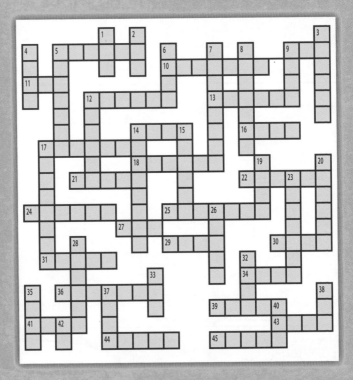

ACROSS

5. food	25. shrimp
9. heaven	27. bread
10. clam	29. squid
11. bar	30. draft beer (North)
12. lunch	31. cellar
13. small coffee with milk	34. water
14. ball	36. strawberry
16. god	39. dish
17. orange	41. pear
18. camel	43. candle
21. grilled bread	44. pasta
22. evening tea or snack	45. fork
24. ear	

DOWN

1. thread	19. toad
2. salt	20. ice cream
3. cheese	23. chair
4. dribble	26. abbot
5. beer	28. onion
6. duck	32. beef
7. flounder	33. walnut
8. toast	35. soup
9. glass	37. tuna
12. roasted	38. tea
14. cod	40. egg
15. plum	42. frog
17. lamprey	

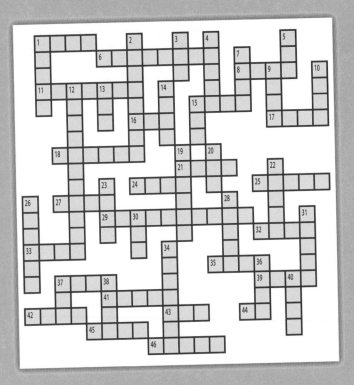

ACROSS

1. duck
6. grilled
8. bear
11. light black coffee
15. coconut
16. heaven
17. spawn
18. banana
21. grapes
24. soft
25. rice
27. dribble
29. beerhouse
32. mush
33. sweet
35. ball
37. medium black coffee
39. ice
41. milk
42. turkey
43. walnut
44. frog
45. hunger
46. cabbage

DOWN

1. pork
2. watermelon
3. salt
4. octopus
5. thread
7. juice
9. toad
10. god
12. restaurant
13. egg
14. tuna
15. tea
19. cheese
20. bread
22. trout
23. knife
26. sandwich
28. litre
30. kidney
31. fork
34. sweet pepper
36. water
37. bar
38. garlic
40. squid

CROSSWORDS

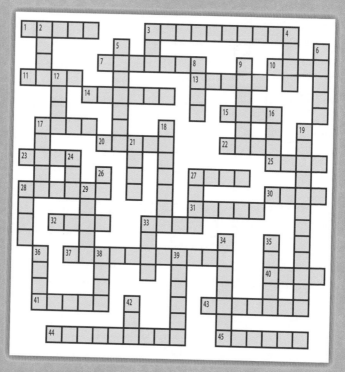

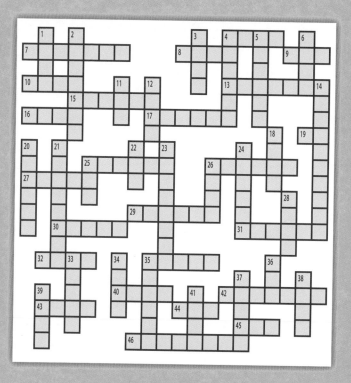

Sleep & Health

8

hotel

barulho - noise
campismo - camping
estalagem - inn
limpeza - cleaning
pensão - boarding house
pousada - heritage inn
residencial - guest house
sono - sleep

WHERE

BEDROOM

ARMÁRIO

CANDEEIRO

LÂMPADA

AQUECIMENTO

ALMOFADA

COBERTOR

ESCADA

ELEVADOR

PAREDE

CORREDOR

COLCHÃO

LENÇOL

CHAVE

CAMA

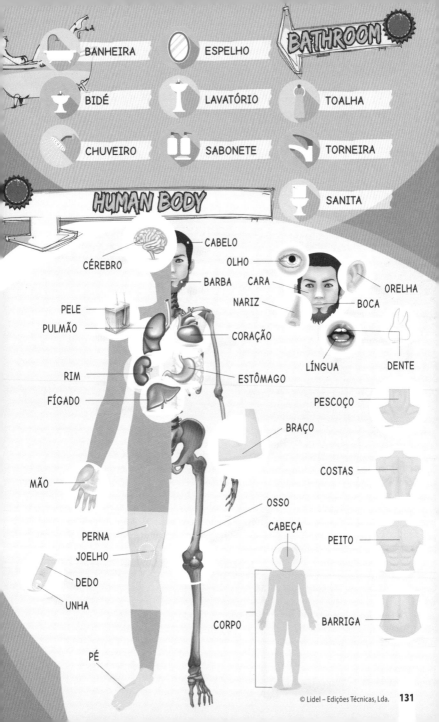

BATHROOM

BANHEIRA

ESPELHO

BIDÉ

LAVATÓRIO

TOALHA

CHUVEIRO

SABONETE

TORNEIRA

SANITA

HUMAN BODY

CÉREBRO

CABELO

OLHO

CARA

ORELHA

BARBA

NARIZ

BOCA

PELE

PULMÃO

CORAÇÃO

LÍNGUA

DENTE

RIM

ESTÔMAGO

FÍGADO

PESCOÇO

BRAÇO

COSTAS

MÃO

OSSO

CABEÇA

PERNA

PEITO

JOELHO

DEDO

UNHA

CORPO

BARRIGA

PÉ

IDIOMS

Dar com a língua nos dentes
"To give with the tongue in the teeth"
To reveal a secret

Fazer das tripas coração
"To make of the guts heart"
To make an enormous effort

Do pé para a mão
"From the foot to the hand"
Out of the blue

Puxar pela cabeça
"To pull for the head"
(To make an effort) to think or remembe

Dar o braço a torcer
"To give the arm to bend"
To accept defeat

Mandar bocas
"To send mouths"
To have a dig at somebody

TROUBLES

Socorro!
Help!

É urgente!
It is urgent!

Já me sinto bem.
I feel good now.

Preciso de uma ambulância.
I need an ambulance.

Preciso de um médico.
I need a doctor.

Sinto-me mal.
I feel bad.

Sinto-me doente.
I feel sick.

Help!

Preciso de ajuda!
I need help!

acidente
emergência

constipação - cold
doença - illness
doente - ill, sick, patient
dor - pain
febre - fever
ferida - wound
gripe - flu
morte - death
sangue - blood
saúde - health
sujo - dirty
tosse - cough
vida - life
vomitar - to throw up

ESPIRRO

ATCHIM!!

HEALERS

ÓCULOS

álcool
creme
hospital
injeção

supositório
termómetro
tratamento
vacina

COMPRIMIDO

consulta - doctor's appointment
receita - prescription
xarope - syrup

LENÇOS

AMBULÂNCIA

CROSSWORDS

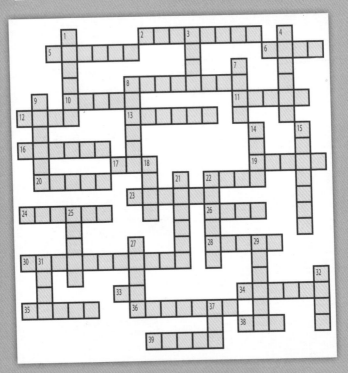

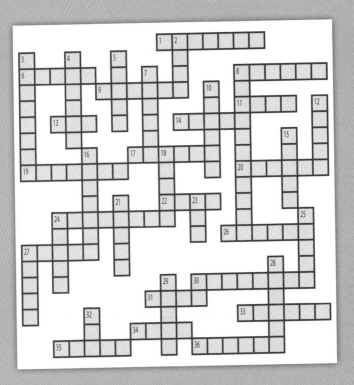

CROSSWORDS

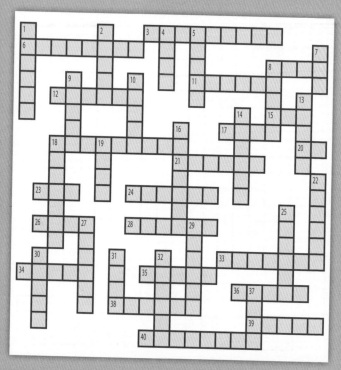

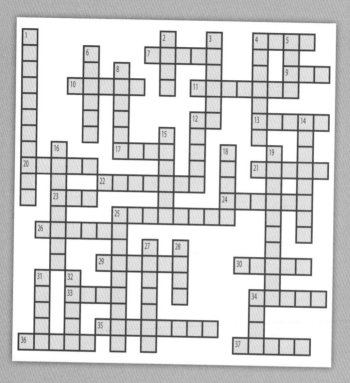

4. bidet
7. beard
9. pain
10. nose
11. help
12. foot
13. flu
17. bone
20. key
21. arm
22. noise
23. hand
24. back
25. stomach
26. glasses
29. wall
30. bath
33. nail
34. body
35. dangerous
36. fever
37. to make

1. cold
2. face
3. syrup
4. belly
5. finger
6. bedroom
8. liver
12. chest
14. to need
15. knee
16. chemist
18. handkerchief
19. treatment
25. inn
27. healer
28. skin
31. cough
32. to pull
34. bed

Shopping & Culture

Shops
Lojas

Press
Imprensa

Money
Dinheiro

Hobbies
Passatempos

Materials
Materiais

Holidays
Feriados

Colours
Cores

Sports
Desportos

Clothes
Roupa

Politics
Política

Gifts & utilities
Prendas e utilidades

Religion
Religião

Mail
Correio

Crosswords
Palavras-cruzadas

9

SHOPS

Quero...
I want...

Não quero...
I don't want...

Queria...
I would like...

Não queria...
I wouldn't like...

CABELEIREIRO

PAPELARIA

BARBEIRO

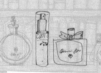

PERFUMARIA

LIVRARIA

SAPATARIA

BANCO

MONEY

Quanto custa?   É caro.   Não tem mais barato?

How much is it?   It's expensive.   Don't you have a cheaper one?

Custa...   É barato.   Onde é a caixa?

It is...   It's cheap.   Where's the cashier?

câmbio - money exchange

compra - buying

compras - shopping

conta - bill

despesa - expense

gorjeta - tip

multibanco - ATM, debit card

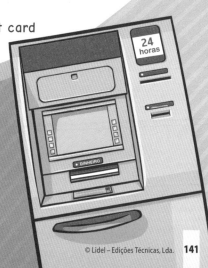

MATERIALS

De que material é feito?
Which material is it made from?

Tem com um material diferente?
Do you have it with a different material?

aço - steel

algodão - cotton

barro - clay

borracha - rubber

cerâmica - pottery

cobre - copper

cortiça - cork

estanho - tin

lã - wool

linho - linen

madeira - wood

ouro - gold

pano - cloth

porcelana - chinaware

prata - silver

tecido - fabric

vidro - glass

pó - powder

alumínio
bronze
cristal
fibra
natural
plástico
puro

COLOURS

De que cor? Tem de outra cor?
Which colour? Do you have it in a different colour?

AMARELO
CINZENTO
PRETO
BRANCO
COR DE LARANJA
ROXO
AZUL
COR-DE-ROSA
ENCARNADO / / VERMELHO
VERDE
CASTANHO

cinzento   > cinza (ash)
encarnado   > carne (flesh, meat)
castanho   > castanha (chestnut)
cor-de-rosa > rosa (rose)

CLOTHES

De que número?	De que tamanho?	Quantos?
Which number?	Which size?	How many?

Tem maior?   Tem mais largo?
Do you have it larger?   Do you have it wider?

Tem mais pequeno?
Do you have it smaller?

BLUSA

BOLSO

BOTA

CALÇAS

CALÇÕES

CAMISA

CAMISOLA

CASACO

CHAPÉU

CINTO

144

CUECAS

PULÔVER

GRAVATA

MANGA

T-SHIRT

GABARDINE

TÉNIS

SAPATOS

SAIA

FATO

SUTIÃ

VESTIDO

GIFTS & UTILITIES

forma - shape
lembrança - souvenir
recordação - souvenir

CADERNO   **CAIXA**   **CANETA**

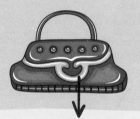

CARTEIRA   **MALA**   **CESTO**

CIGARRO   COLA   **BONECO   FOTOGRAFIA**

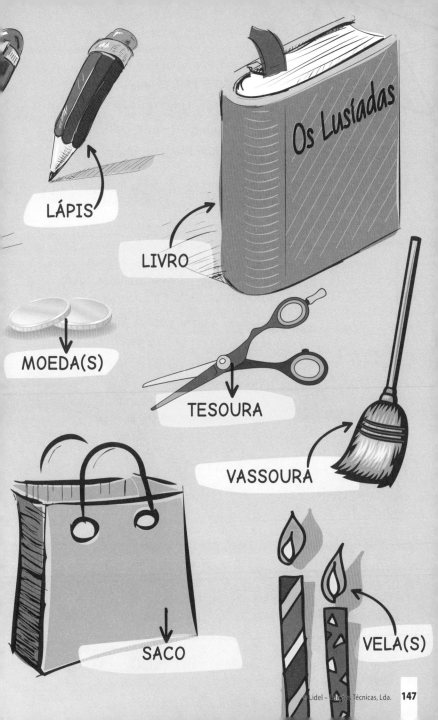

LÁPIS

LIVRO

Os Lusíadas

MOEDA(S)

TESOURA

VASSOURA

SACO

VELA(S)

MAIL

assunto - subject

chamada - (phone) call

telefonema - phone call

telemóvel - mobile phone

40
LISBOA

Onde são os Correios?
Where's the post office?

Tenho correio?
Any mail for me?

Quero selos para um postal para a Suécia.
I want stamps for a postcard to Sweden.

Quero selos para cartas.
I want stamps for letters.

GUICHÉ

GUICHÉ

CORREIOS 1

CORREIOS 2

BALCÃO

MORADA, REMETENTE

SELO

ENVELOPE

DESTINATÁRIO

CARTA

ENCOMENDA

João Pedro

ASSINATURA

CORREIO

MARCO DO CORREIO

TELEFONE

PRESS

Tem jornais estrangeiros?
Do you have foreign newspapers?

Quero uma revista sobre...
I want a magazine about...

notícia(s) - news

CYBERTALK

dd tc.
k fazes :)

tou kasa a tua
espera lolada

Donde teclas?
Que fazes?

Estou em casa à tua
espera. (gargalhada)

Where do you type from?
What are you doing?

I am at home waiting
for you. (LOL)

JORNAL

REVISTA

RÁDIO

TELEVISÃO

Jornais portugueses em língua estrangeira

Besides foreign press, you can find local newspapers in English, Russian, Romanian and Mandarin.

HOBBIES

baile - ball
canção - song
colégio - private school
costume - habit
divertimentos - pastime
escola - school
espetáculo - show
feira - fair, street market

férias - holidays
festa - party
leitura - reading
letra (música) - lyrics
passatempo - hobby
pintura - painting
poesia - poetry
quadro - painting, picture

arte
ciência
cinema
circo
coleção
concerto
cultura
dança
estilo
filme
história
literatura
música
teatro
universidade

BANDA

BANDA DESENHADA

CARICATURA

DESENHO

GIRA-DISCOS

EXPOSIÇÃO

DISCO

DISCOTECA

VINDIMA

TOURADA

XADREZ

IDIOMS

Pegar o touro pelos cornos
"To hold the bull by the horns"
To face a problem directly

Ficar nos cornos do touro
"To stay in the horns of the bull"
To take responsibility that is supposed to be shared

TIP

Most foreign movies both on TV
and at the cinema are subtitled.

FADO

The word means fate or destiny. Its origin is controversial. Some say the music is of African origin and arrived from Brazil in the early 19th century. It became a symbol of national culture during the 20th century.

Its most renowned singer is Amália Rodrigues (1920-1999).

GAIVOTA

Se uma gaivota viesse
Trazer-me o céu de Lisboa
No desenho que fizesse
Nesse céu onde o olhar
É uma asa que não voa,
Esmorece e cai no mar

Que perfeito coração
No meu peito bateria,
Meu amor na tua mão,
Nessa mão onde cabia
Perfeito o meu coração.

Se um português marinheiro,
Dos sete mares andarilho
Fosse quem sabe o primeiro
A contar o que inventasse,
Se um olhar de novo brilho
No meu olhar se enlaçasse

Que perfeito coração
No meu peito bateria,
Meu amor na tua mão,
Nessa mão onde cabia
Perfeito o meu coração

Se ao dizer adeus à vida,
As aves todas do céu
Me dessem na despedida
O teu olhar derradeiro,
Esse olhar que era só teu,
Amor que foste o primeiro

Que perfeito coração
Morreria no meu peito,
Meu amor na tua mão,
Nessa mão onde perfeito
Bateu o meu coração.

(Música: Alain Oulman
Letra: Alexandre O'Neill)

SEAGULL

If a seagull would come
To bring me the sky of Lisbon
In the drawing it would make,
In that sky where the look
Is a wing that does not fly,
Fades and falls in the sea

What a perfect heart
In my chest would beat,
My love in your hand
In that hand where it fitted
Perfect my heart

If a Portuguese sailor
Wonderer of the seven seas
Would be, who knows, the first
To tell what he would invent
If a look of new brightness
Would intermingle in my look

What a perfect heart
In my chest would beat,
My love in your hand
In that hand where it fitted
Perfect my heart

If when I'd say goodbye to life
All the birds of the sky
Would offer me for farewell
Your very last look,
That look that was only yours
You who were my first love

What a perfect heart
Would die in my chest
My love in your hand
In that hand where perfect
Had beaten my heart.

PORTUGAL

154

HOLIDAYS

Popular street festivals in June that welcome summer and celebrate three Christian saints. Each one of them is a local holiday in several different cities. For instance, Santo António (13th) in Lisboa, São João (24th) in Porto and Braga, and São Pedro (29th) in Sintra. The main festivity takes places the evening before.

SANTOS POPULARES

✓ PÁSCOA

✓ NATAL

✓ CARNAVAL

desporto - sports
equipa - team
jogo - game, match

SPORTS

FUTEBOL

ANDEBOL

ATLETISMO

BASQUETEBOL

GOLO

BILHAR

BOLA

GINÁSTICA

CAÇA

NATAÇÃO

POLITICS

desemprego - unemployment
desenvolvimento - development
ditadura - dictatorship
greve - strike
guerra - war
lei - law
paz - peace
poder - power

comunismo
democracia
fascismo
governo
ministro
justiça
liberdade

RELIGION

ateu - atheist
batizado - christening
bispo - bishop
deus - god
judeu - Jew
missa - mass
muçulmano - Muslim
padre - priest
sagrado - sacred

budista
católico
cristão
espírita
protestante

Santos

são – saint + consonnant (masc.) = São João or S. João
santo – saint + vowel (masc.) = Santo António or S. António
santa – saint (fem.) = Santa Maria or S. Maria

CROSSWORDS

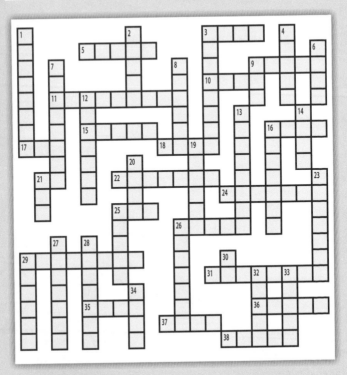

ACROSS

3. shop
5. fibre
9. bill
10. violet
11. souvenir
15. record
16. god
17. law
18. hunting
21. powder
22. habit
24. science
25. saint (masc.)
26. bull
29. grey
31. fascism
35. atheist
36. bank
37. glue
38. coin

DOWN

1. material
2. silver
3. book shop
4. tennis
6. cloth
7. religion
8. guard
9. colour
12. wood
13. Roman catholic
14. gold
16. drawing
19. exchange
20. boot
21. peace
23. notebook
25. saint (masc.)
26. size
27. handball
28. holiday
29. cinema
30. wool
32. copper
33. saint (fem.)
34. pure

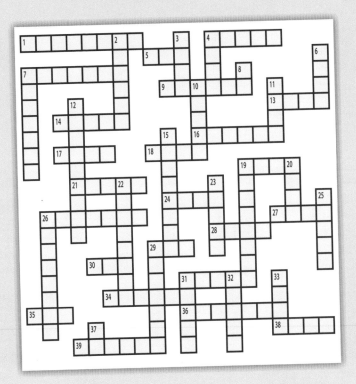

ACROSS

1. Roman catholic	24. art
4. blouse	26. wood
5. saint (masc.)	27. bag
7. shorts	28. atheist
9. shoe	29. colour
13. gold	30. law
14. glass	31. saint (masc.)
16. fabric	34. pen
17. candle	35. peace
18. cloth	36. natural
19. god	38. blue
21. record	39. cheap

DOWN

2. jacket	22. wallet
3. shop	23. to hold
4. boot	25. horn
6. goal	26. material
7. collection	29. notebook
8. powder	31. saint (fem.)
10. black	32. bull
11. violet	33. ball
12. liberty	37. wool
15. brown	
19. money	
20. skirt	

CROSSWORDS

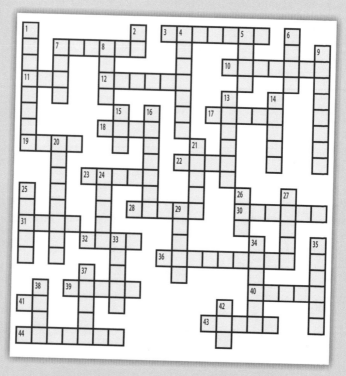

3. holiday
7. poetry
10. culture
11. colour
12. buying
17. book
18. cloth
19. gold
22. ball
23. strike
28. saint (fem.)
30. team
31. skirt
32. suit
36. liberty
39. fibre
40. ball
41. powder
43. larger
44. shopping

1. fascism
2. wool
4. tin
5. god
6. blue
7. pure
8. bag
9. broom
13. billiards
14. bill
15. peace
16. tip
20. religion
21. coin
24. clothes
25. party
26. law
27. film
29. tennis
33. bull
34. exchange
35. number
37. to stay
38. game
42. saint (masc.)

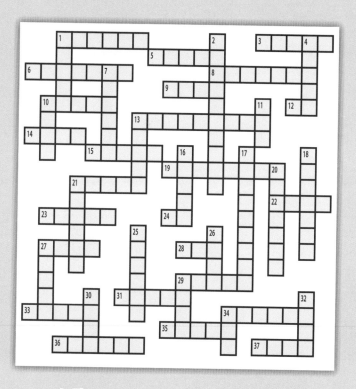

ACROSS

1. music	22. atheist
3. record	23. tennis
5. copper	24. wool
6. justice	27. bag
8. shorts	28. peace
9. expensive	29. film
10. dance	31. sleeve
12. powder	33. bill
13. raincoat	34. shirt
14. pure	35. pocket
15. Jewish	36. guard
19. pottery	37. gun
21. ball	

DOWN

1. mass	26. blue
2. souvenir	27. saint (masc.)
4. basket	29. suit
7. hat	30. skirt
10. god	32. hunting
11. law	34. colour
13. strike	
16. party	
17. different	
18. notebook	
20. yellow	
21. puppet	
25. pants	

Literature

10

The Lusiads, Luís de Camões

CANTO PRIMEIRO

As armas e os barões assinalados,
Que da ocidental praia lusitana,
Por mares nunca dantes navegados,
Passaram ainda além da Taprobana,
Em perigos e guerras esforçados
Mais do que prometia a força humana,
E entre gente remota edificaram
Novo Reino que tanto sublimaram;

E também as memórias gloriosas
Daqueles reis que foram dilatando
A Fé, o Império, e as terras viciosas
De África e de Ásia andaram devastando;
E aqueles que por obras valerosas
Se vão da lei da morte libertando
- Cantando espalharei por toda a parte,
Se a tanto me ajudar o engenho e arte.

Luís de Camões, in **Os Lusíadas** (1572)

CANTO ONE

Arms are my theme, and those matchless heroes
Who from Portugal's far western shores
By oceans where none had ventured
Voyaged to Taprobana and beyond,
Enduring hazards and assaults
Such as drew on more than human prowess
Among far distant peoples, to proclaim
A New Age and win undying fame;

Kings likewise of glorious memory
Who magnified Christ and Empire,
Bringing ruin on the degenerate
Lands of Africa and Asia;
And other whose immortal deeds
Have conquered death's oblivion
- These words will go wherever there are men
If art and invention steer my pen.

Translated by Landeg White
(**The Lusiads**, Oxford University Press, 2008)

"Portuguese Sea"
Fernando Pessoa

MAR PORTUGUÊS

Ó mar salgado, quanto do teu sal
São lágrimas de Portugal!
Por te cruzarmos, quantas mães choraram,
Quantos filhos em vão rezaram!
Quantas noivas ficaram por casar
Para que fosses nosso, ó mar!

Valeu a pena? Tudo vale a pena
Se a alma não é pequena.
Quem quer passar além do Bojador
Tem que passar além da dor.
Deus ao mar o perigo e o abismo deu,
Mas nele é que espelhou o céu.

Fernando Pessoa, in *Mensagem* (1934)

PORTUGUESE SEA

O salty Sea, how much of your salt
Are tears from Portugal!
Because we sailed you, how many mothers did weep,
How many children prayed in vain!
How many brides were left unmarried?
For you to be ours, oh Sea!

Was it worth it? Everything is worth it
If the soul is not small.
Who wants to pass beyond Cape Bojador
Must go beyond pain.
To the Sea, God gave danger and abyss,
Yet in it did He mirror the sky.

BALTASAR AND BLIMUNDA,
José Saramago

Procura cada qual, por seu próprio caminho, a graça, seja ela o que for, uma simples paisagem com algum céu por cima, uma hora do dia ou da noite, duas árvores, três se forem as de Rembrandt, um murmúrio, sem sabermos se com isto se fecha o caminho ou finalmente se abre, e para onde, para outra paisagem, ou hora, ou árvore, um murmúrio, veja-se este padre que anda a tirar de si um Deus e a pôr outro, mal sabendo que proveito haverá na troca, e, se proveito houver, quem dele finalmente aproveitará, veja-se este músico que outra música que esta não saberia compor, que não estará vivo daqui a cem anos para ouvir a primeira sinfonia do homem, erradamente chamada Nona, veja-se este soldado maneta que, por ironia dos acasos, é fabricante de asas, nunca tendo passado da infantaria, alguma vez sabe o homem o que o espera, este menos que qualquer outro, veja-se a mulher dos olhos excessivos, que para descobrir vontades nasceu, não passavam de peloticas e bufarinhices as suas demonstrações de tumor, feto estrangulado e moeda de prata, agora, sim, é que se irão ver as obras maiores do seu destino, quando o padre Bartolomeu Lourenço chegar à quinta de S. Sebastião da Pedreira e disser, Blimunda, está Lisboa atormentada de uma grande doença, morrem pessoas em todas as casas, lembrei-me de que não teremos melhor ocasião para recolher as vontades dos moribundos,

Every man follows his own path in search of grace, whatever that grace may be, a simple landscape with the sky overhead, a certain hour of the day or night, two trees, three if they are painted by Rembrandt, a sigh, without knowing whether this closes or finally opens the path or where the path may lead us, whether to some other landscape, hour, tree, or sigh. Behold this priest who is about to cast out one God and replace Him with another, without knowing whether this new allegiance will do him any good in the end. Behold this musician who would find it impossible to compose any other kind of music and who will no longer be alive a hundred years from now to hear the first symphony, which is mistakenly referred to as the Ninth Symphony. Behold this one-handed soldier who has ironically become manufacturer of wings, although he has never risen to being more than a common foot soldier. Man rarely knows what to expect from life, and this man least of all. Behold this woman with those extraordinary eyes, who was born to perceive wills. Her revelations about a tumor, a strangled fetus, and a silver coin were mere child's play when compared with the wonders she is destined to achieve when Padre Bartolomeu Lourenço returns to the estate of São Sebastião da Pedreira and tells her: Blimunda, Lisbon is stricken by a horrendous plague. People are dying everywhere. It has just occurred to me that this is an excellent opportunity to collect wills from the dying,

se as conservam ainda, mas é meu dever avisar-te de que correrás grandes perigos, não vais se não quiseres, nem eu te obrigaria, ainda que obrigar-te estivesse na minha mão, Que doença é essa, Dizem que foi trazida por uma nau do Brasil e que primeiro se manifestou na Ericeira. A minha terra fica perto, disse Baltasar, e o padre respondeu, Não há notícia de ter morrido gente em Mafra, mas, sobre a doença, pelos sinais que dá, é vómito negro ou febre amarela, o nome pouco importa, o caso é que estão morrendo como tordos, que decides tu Blimunda. Levantou-se Blimunda do mocho onde estava sentada, ergueu a tampa da arca e lá de dentro tirou o frasco de vidro, quantas vontades ali haveria, talvez umas cem, quase nada para as necessidades, e mesmo assim fora uma longa e custosa caçada, muito jejum, às vezes perdida num labirinto, onde está a vontade que a não vejo, só vísceras e ossos, a rede agónica dos nervos, o mar de sangue, a comida pastosa no estômago, o excremento final, Irás, perguntou o padre, Irei, respondeu ela, Mas não sozinha, disse Baltasar.

José Saramago, in *Memorial do Convento* (Editorial Caminho, 1982)

(pp. 178-179)

if their wills are intact. But I must warn you that you will face great danger. Don't go unless you really want to go, for I shall put you under no obligation, even though it is within my power to do so.

- What is the plague?

- It is rumored that the plague was carried here by passengers aboard a ship from Brazil and it first broke out in Ericeira.

- That's close to my home town, said Baltasar, whereupon the priest reassured him: No deaths have been reported in Mafra. Judging from the symptoms, the disease is believed to be the black plague or yellow fever. The name scarcely matters. The fact is that people are dying like flies. You must decide, Blimunda.

She got up from her stool, raised the lid of the chest, and brought out a glass phial. How many wills were in there? she wondered. About a hundred, perhaps, but certainly nothing like the number they required. And even this amount had required a lengthy and arduous search and a great deal of fasting, often to find oneself lost as in a labyrinth: Where is that will? All I can see are entrails and bones, an agonizing maze of nerves, a sea of blood, viscous food lodged in the stomach before finally turning to excrement.

- Will you go? the priest asked her.

- I shall go, she replied.

- But not on your own, Baltasar added.

José Saramago, in ***Baltasar and Blimunda*** (Jonathan Cape, 1988)

(pp. 161-162)

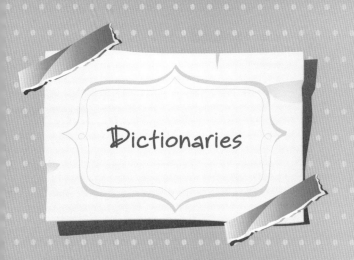

Dictionaries

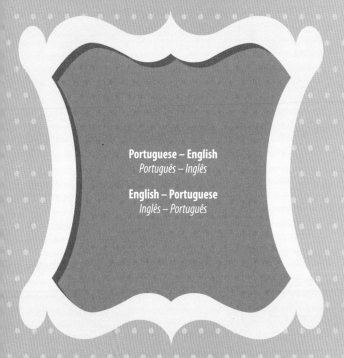

Portuguese – English
Português – Inglês

English – Portuguese
Inglês – Português

11

PORTUGUESE	ENGLISH	YOUR LANGUAGE
A		
a	to	
a, as	the (fem.)	
abade	abbot	
abelha	bee	
abraço	hug	
abril	April	
ação	action	
achar	to find	
acidente	accident	
aço	steel	
açúcar	sugar	
adega	cellar	
adeus	goodbye	
adorar	to worship, to love	
advogado	lawyer	
aeroporto	airport	
agora	now	
agosto	August	
agricultor	farmer	
água	water	
aguaceiro	shower	
aguardente	brandy	
águia	eagle	
aí	there (near)	
ajuda	help	
albatroz, alcatraz	albatross	
álcool	alcohol	
aldeia	village	
alegre	happy	
alegria	joy, happiness	
alemão	German	
alface	lettuce	
alfândega	customs	
algodão	cotton	
alho	garlic	
ali	there (far)	
almoço	lunch	
almofada	pillow	
alto	tall; loud	
alumínio	aluminium	
alunar	to land on the moon	
amanhã	tomorrow	
amar	to love	
amarar	to land on water	
amarelo	yellow	
ambiente	environment	

PORTUGUESE	ENGLISH	YOUR LANGUAGE
ambulância	ambulance	
amêijoa	clam	
ameixa	plum	
amêndoa	almond	
amendoim	peanut	
americano	American	
amigo	friend	
amor	love	
ananás	pineapple	
andar	to walk; to ride	
andebol	handball	
andorinha	swallow	
anedota	joke	
animal	animal	
anjo	angel	
ano	year	
antes	before	
ao lado de	next to	
apanhar	to catch	
apelido	family name	
aquecimento	heating	
aqui	here	
aquilo	that (far)	
ar	air	
árabe	Arab, Arabic	
aranha	spider	
área	area	
armário	wardrobe	
armazém	store	
arquiteto	architect	
arroz	rice	
arte	art	
artista	artist	
árvore	tree	
assado	roasted	
assinatura	signature	
assunto	subject	
até	untill	
atenção	attention	
ateu	atheist	
atitude	attitude	
atletismo	athletics	
atrás	behind, back	
atum	tuna	
autocarro	bus	
avenida	avenue	
avião	plane, airplane	
avô	grandfather	
avó	grandmother	
avós	grandparents	

PORTUGUESE	ENGLISH	YOUR LANGUAGE
azeite	olive oil	
azeitona	olive	
azul	blue	

B

PORTUGUESE	ENGLISH	YOUR LANGUAGE
baba	dribble, mousse (old)	
bacalhau	cod	
bagaço	brandy	
bagagem	luggage	
baile	ball	
bairro	neighbourhood	
baixo	short	
balcão	desk	
bambu	bamboo	
banana	banana	
banco	bank	
banda	band	
banda desenhada	comics	
banheira	bathtub	
bar	bar	
barato	cheap	
barba	beard	
barbeiro	barber's	
barco	boat	
barragem	dam, reservoir	
barriga	belly	
barro	clay	
barroco	baroque	
barulho	noise	
basquetebol	basketball	
batata	potato	
batizado	christening	
batuque	drum	
bebé	baby	
bebida	drink	
beijo	kiss	
beira-mar	seaside	
beleza	beauty	
belga	Belgian	
bem	well, good	
bica	medium black coffee, espresso	
bicicleta	bicycle	
bidé	bidet	
bife	steak; brit (slang)	
bilhar	billiards	
bilhete	ticket	
bilheteira	ticket office	
biombo	screen	
bispo	bishop	

PORTUGUESE	ENGLISH	YOUR LANGUAGE
blusa	blouse	
boca	mouth	
bocado	bit	
boi	ox	
bola	ball	
bolacha	biscuit	
bolo	cake	
bolso	pocket	
bom, boa	good	
bomba de gasolina	gas station	
boneco	puppet	
bonito	beautiful	
bora (slang)	let's go	
borboleta	butterfly	
borracha	rubber	
bota	boot	
braço	arm	
branco	white	
brazuca (slang)	Brazilian	
brincadeira	fun	
bronze	bronze	
budista	Buddhist	
bué (slang)	very	
burro	donkey	

C

PORTUGUESE	ENGLISH	YOUR LANGUAGE
cabeça	head	
cabeleireiro	hairdresser	
cabelo	hair	
cabo-verdiano	Capeverdean	
cabra	goat	
cabrito	goatling	
caça	hunting	
cachorro	hotdog	
cadeira	chair	
caderno	notebook	
café	coffee, café	
café duplo	large black coffee	
caixa	box; cashier	
caju	cashew	
calças	trousers	
calções	shorts	
calendário	calendar	
calor	heat	
cama	bed	
camarão	shrimp	
câmbio	money exchange	
camelo	camel	
camião	truck	
caminho	way	

PORTUGUESE	ENGLISH	YOUR LANGUAGE
camioneta	coach	
camisa	shirt	
camisola	sweater	
camone (slang)	foreigner	
campismo	camping	
campo	countryside; field	
canção	song	
candeeiro	lamp	
caneca	large draught beer	
caneta	pen	
cantar	to sing	
cão	dog	
capela	chapel	
cara	face	
caraças (slang)	masks, heck	
caracol	snail	
caralho (slang)	cock	
caranguejo	crab	
carapau	horse mackerel	
caricatura	cartoon	
carioca	light black coffee	
carnaval	carnival	
carne	meat; flesh	
carneiro	lamb	
caro	expensive	
carpinteiro	carpenter	
carro	car	
carroça	cart	
carta	letter	
carteira	wallet	
carvalho	oak	
casa	house	
casa de banho	bathroom	
casaco	jacket	
casal	couple	
casamento	wedding	
castanha	chestnut	
castanheiro	chestnut	
castanho	brown	
catedral	cathedral	
católico	Roman Catholic	
catorze	fourteen	
cavalo	horse	
cebola	onion	
cedilha	Small comma sign in letter ç	
cedo	early	
cem	hundred	
cenoura	carrot	
centeio	rye	
cento	hundred	

PORTUGUESE	ENGLISH	YOUR LANGUAGE
centro comercial	shopping center	
cerâmica	pottery	
cereal	cereal	
cérebro	brain	
cereja	cherry	
certeza	certainty, sure	
cerveja	beer	
cervejaria	beer house	
cesto	basket	
céu	sky; heaven	
chá	tea	
chamada	(phone) call	
chamar	to call	
champô	shampoo	
chapéu	hat	
charro (slang)	joint	
chatice	boredom	
chave	key	
chávena	cup	
checo	Czech	
chefe	chief	
chegada	arrival	
cheiro	smell	
chocolate	chocolate	
chuva	rain	
chuveiro	shower	
cidade	city	
ciência	science	
cigano	gipsy, Romani	
cigarro	cigarette	
cimbalino	medium black coffee, espresso (North)	
cinco	five	
cinema	cinema	
cinquenta	fifty	
cinto	belt	
cinza	ash	
cinzento	grey	
circo	circus	
classe	class	
clube	club	
cobertor	blanket	
cobra	snake, cobra	
cobre	copper	
coco	coconut	
coelho	rabbit	
cola	glue	
colchão	mattress	
coleção	collection	
colega	colleague	

PORTUGUESE	ENGLISH	YOUR LANGUAGE
colégio	private school	
colher	spoon	
com	with	
comboio	train	
comerciante	trader	
comida	food	
como	how	
companhia	company	
competição	competition	
completamente	completly	
complicado	tricky	
compra	buying	
compras	shopping	
compreender	to understand	
comprimido	pill	
computador	computer	
comunismo	communism	
concerto	concert	
conhecer	to know	
constipação	cold	
construção	construction	
consulta	doctor's appointment	
conta	bill	
contrário	contrary	
controlo	control, check	
convento	convent	
conversa	conversation, talk	
convite	invitation	
copo	glass	
cor	colour	
coração	heart	
cor de laranja	orange	
cor-de-rosa	pink	
corno	horn	
corpo	body	
corredor	corridor	
correio	mail	
correios	post office	
costas	back	
costume	habit	
couve	cabbage	
cozido	boiled	
cozinha	kitchen	
cravo	carnation	
creme	cream	
criança	child	
cristal	crystal	
cristão	Christian	
cruzamento	crossroad	
cuecas	pants	

PORTUGUESE	ENGLISH	YOUR LANGUAGE
cuidado	care	
cultura	culture	
cumprimentos	address, greetings	
cunhada	sister-in-law	
cunhado	brother-in-law	
custar	to cost	

D

PORTUGUESE	ENGLISH	YOUR LANGUAGE
dado	dice	
dança	dance	
dar	to give	
data	date	
de	of	
dedo	finger, toe	
democracia	democracy	
dente	tooth	
dentro	inside	
depois	after	
deputado	member of parliament	
desbundar (slang)	to revel	
descida	way down	
descobrimento	discovery	
desculpe	sorry	
desde	since	
desemprego	unemployment	
desenho	drawing	
desenrascanço (slang)	resourcefulness	
desenvolvimento	development	
desgosto	grief	
despesa	expense	
desporto	sport	
destinatário	addressee	
destino	destination	
deus	god	
devagar	slow	
dez	ten	
dezanove	nineteen	
dezasseis	sixteen	
dezassete	seventeen	
dezembro	December	
dezoito	eighteen	
dia	day	
diálogo	dialogue	
dicionário	dictionary	
diferença	difference	
diferente	different	
difícil	difficult	
dificuldade	difficulty	
dinamarquês	Danish	

PORTUGUESE	ENGLISH	YOUR LANGUAGE
dinheiro	money	
direção	direction	
direita	right	
direto	direct	
disco	record	
discoteca	disco	
distância	distance	
ditadura	dictatorship	
divertimentos	pastime	
dizer	to say	
doce	sweet	
documento	document	
doença	illness	
doente	patient, ill, sick	
dois	two	
domingo	Sunday	
dona	lady	
dono	owner	
dor	pain	
doutor	doctor, person with a degree, important person	
doze	twelve	
dragão	dragon	
dúvida	doubt	
duzentos	two hundred	

E

e	and	
edifício	building	
ela	she, it	
elas	they (fem.)	
ele	he, it	
elefante	elephant	
eles	they (masc.)	
eletricista	electrician	
elétrico	tram	
elevador	lift	
em	in, on, at	
em frente	ahead	
embora	away	
emergência	emergency	
emprego	job	
empresa	firm	
empurrar	to push	
encarnado	red	
encomenda	order, parcel	
encontro	meeting	
enfermeiro	nurse	
engenheiro	engineer	
engolir	to swallow	

PORTUGUESE	ENGLISH	YOUR LANGUAGE
enquanto	while	
entrada	entrance	
entre	between	
envelope	envelope	
equipa	team	
erva (slang)	weed	
escada	stair	
escola	school	
escrever	to write	
escritório	office	
espanhol	Spanish	
espetáculo	show	
espelho	mirror	
espera	waiting	
esperar	to wait	
espírito	spirit	
espirro	sneeze	
esquecer	to forget	
esquerda	left	
essencialmente	essentially	
estação	station; season	
estádio	stadium	
estado	state	
estalagem	inn	
estanho	tin	
estar	to be (less permanent)	
estátua	statue	
este	east	
estilo	style	
estômago	stomach	
estrada	road	
estrangeiro	foreign; foreigner	
estudante	student	
etiqueta	tag	
eu	I, me	
eucalipto	eucalyptus	
exame	examination	
exposição	exhibition	
expressão	phrase	
extraordinário	extraordinary	

F

PORTUGUESE	ENGLISH	YOUR LANGUAGE
fábrica	factory	
faca	knife	
fácil	easy	
falar	to speak	
família	family	
farinha	flour	
farmácia	chemist	
fascismo	fascism	

PORTUGUESE	ENGLISH	YOUR LANGUAGE
fato	suit	
favor	favour	
fazer	to do	
febre	fever	
feijão	bean	
feio	ugly	
feira	fair, street market	
feitiço	witchcraft	
feriado	holiday	
férias	holidays	
ferida	wound	
festa	party	
fetiche	fetish	
fevereiro	February	
fibra	fiber	
ficar	to stay	
fígado	liver	
figo	fig	
figura	picture	
fila	queue, line	
filha	daughter	
filho	son	
filme	film	
fim de semana	weekend	
finalmente	finally	
finlandês	Finnish	
fino	thin, regular draught beer (North)	
fio	thread	
fixe (slang)	cool	
flor	flower	
foda-se	fuck it	
fogo (slang)	hell	
fome	hunger	
fonte	fountain	
fora	outside	
forma	shape	
formiga	ant	
forte	strong	
fotografia	photo	
foz	mouth	
fraco	weak	
francês	French	
franciú (slang)	French person	
frango	chicken	
frase	sentence	
freira	nun	
frente	front	
fresco	cool	
frio	cold	

PORTUGUESE	ENGLISH	YOUR LANGUAGE
frito	fried	
fruta	fruit (in general)	
fruto	(single) fruit	
fundação	foundation	
futebol	football	
futuro	future	

G

PORTUGUESE	ENGLISH	YOUR LANGUAGE
gabardine	raincoat	
gaivota	seagull	
gajo (slang)	guy / bloke	
galão	large coffee with milk	
galego	Galician	
galinha	hen	
galo	cock	
garagem	garage	
garfo	fork	
gargalhada	laughter	
garoto	small coffee with milk	
garrafa	bottle	
gato	cat	
geada	frost	
gelado	ice cream	
gelo	ice	
genro	son-in-law	
gente	people	
geral	general	
gin	gin	
ginástica	gymnastics	
ginja	black cherry	
gira-discos	record player	
giro	cute, nice	
globalizar	to globalise	
golo	goal	
gordo	fat	
gorjeta	tip	
gostar	to like	
governo	government	
gramática	grammar	
grande	big	
gravata	tie	
grego	Greek	
grelhado	grilled	
grelo	cabbage sprout	
greve	strike	
gringo (slang)	American person	
gripe	flu	
grosso	thick	
guardanapo	napkin	
guerra	war	

PORTUGUESE	ENGLISH	YOUR LANGUAGE
guia	guide	
guiché	desk, ticket window	
guineense	Guinean	

H

PORTUGUESE	ENGLISH	YOUR LANGUAGE
haver	to have	
haxe (slang)	hashish	
hebraico	hebrew	
hindi	hindi	
hipopótamo	hippopotamus	
história	history, story	
hoje	today	
homem	man	
hora	hour	
horário	timetable, schedule	
hospital	hospital	
hotel	hotel	
humano	human	
humidade	humidity	
húngaro	Hungarian	

I

PORTUGUESE	ENGLISH	YOUR LANGUAGE
ibérico	Iberian	
ida	going	
idade	age	
igreja	church	
igual	same	
igualmente	likewise	
imperial	regular draught beer	
império	empire	
implementar	to implement	
importante	important	
impossível	impossible	
imprensa	press	
infinito	infinite	
inglês	English	
injeção	injection	
intenção	intention	
interessante	interesting	
inverno	winter	
ir	to go	
irmã	sister	
irmão	brother	
isso	that (near)	
isto	this	
italiana	short espresso	
italiano	Italian	

J

PORTUGUESE	ENGLISH	YOUR LANGUAGE
já	already	

PORTUGUESE	ENGLISH	YOUR LANGUAGE
janeiro	January	
janela	window	
jantar	dinner	
japonês	Japanese	
jardim	garden	
jesuíta	Jesuit	
joelho	knee	
jogo	game, match	
jornal	newspaper	
jornalista	journalist	
jovem	teenager	
judeu	Jew, Jewish	
juiz	judge	
julho	July	
junho	June	
justiça	justice	

L

lã	wool	
lago	lake	
lagosta	lobster	
lâmpada	bulb	
lampreia	lamprey	
lanche	snack or mid-afternoon snack or evening tea	
lápis	pencil	
laranja	orange	
largo	small square; wide	
latim	Latin	
lavabos	toilets	
lavatório	washbasin	
leão	lion	
lebre	hare	
legume	vegetable	
lei	law	
leitão	piglet	
leite	milk	
leitura	reading	
lembrança	souvenir	
lenço	handkerchief	
lençol	sheet	
lento	slow	
leonês	Leonese	
leste	east	
letra	letter, lyrics	
leve	light	
liberdade	liberty, freedom	
licença	excuse	
líder	leader	
limão	lemon	

PORTUGUESE	ENGLISH	YOUR LANGUAGE
limpeza	cleaning	
língua	language, tongue	
língua gestual portuguesa (LGP)	Portuguese sign language	
linguado	flounder	
linha	line, platform	
linho	linen	
literatura	literature	
litro	liter	
lituano	Lithuanian	
livraria	bookshop	
livro	book	
lixo	garbage	
lobo	wolf	
logo	later	
loja	shop	
longe	far	
louro	blond	
lua	moon	
lula	squid	
lusofonia	group of all people who speak Portuguese	

M

PORTUGUESE	ENGLISH	YOUR LANGUAGE
maçã	apple	
macaco	monkey	
madeira	wood	
madrinha	godmother	
mãe	mother	
magro	slim	
maio	May	
maior	bigger	
mais	more	
mal	badly	
mala	suitcase, purse	
malaio	Malay	
malmequer	daisy	
mandar	to send	
mandarim	Mandarin	
manga	sleeve, mango	
manhã	morning	
manteiga	butter	
mão	hand	
mapa	map	
mar	sea	
março	March	
marco do correio	postbox	
maré	tide	
maremoto	tsunami	
maresia	sea smell	

PORTUGUESE	ENGLISH	YOUR LANGUAGE
margem	bank	
marido	husband	
marinha	navy	
marinheiro	sailor	
marisco	seafood	
marisqueira	seafood restaurant	
marítimo	maritime	
marmelada	marmalade	
marmelo	quince	
marulhar	sea sound	
mas	but	
massa	pasta	
material	material	
mau	bad	
máximo	maximum	
mecânico	mechanic	
médico	doctor	
medo	fear	
meia de leite	medium coffee with milk	
meio	middle, means	
mel	honey	
melaço	molasses	
melancia	watermelon	
melão	melon	
melhor	better	
meloa	cantaloupe	
mentira	lie	
menu	menu	
mercado	market	
mercearia	grocer's	
merda (slang)	shit	
mês	month	
mesa	table	
metade	half	
metro	underground, tube	
meu (masc.)	my, mine	
mil	thousand	
milhão	million	
milho	corn	
ministro	minister	
minuto	minute	
mirandês	Mirandese	
missa	mass	
moçárabe	Mozarabic	
mochila	backpack	
moeda	coin	
moinho	mill	
mole	soft	
momento	moment	
monetário	monetary	
monte	hill	

PORTUGUESE	ENGLISH	YOUR LANGUAGE
monumento	monument	
morada	address	
morango	strawberry	
moreno	brunette	
morrer	to die	
morte	death	
mosca	fly	
mosquito	mosquito	
mostrar	to show	
mota	motorbike	
muçulmano	muslim	
muito	much, very	
muitos	many	
mulher	woman, wife	
multibanco	ATM, debit card	
museu	museum	
música	music	

N

PORTUGUESE	ENGLISH	YOUR LANGUAGE
nada	nothing	
namorada	girlfriend	
namorado	boyfriend	
não	no, not	
nariz	nose	
natação	swimming	
natal	Christmas	
natas	cream	
natural	natural	
neta	granddaughter	
neto	grandson	
neve	snow	
nevoeiro	fog	
noite	night, evening after sunset	
noivo	fiancé	
nome	name	
nora	daughter-in-law	
norte	north	
nós	we	
notícia	news	
notícias	news	
nove	nine	
novecentos	nine hundred	
novembro	November	
noventa	ninety	
novo	new	
noz	walnut, nut	
nublado	cloudy	
número	number	
nunca	never	
nuvem	cloud	

PORTUGUESE	ENGLISH	YOUR LANGUAGE
O		
o, os	the (masc.)	
obrigado	thanks	
obviamente	obviously	
ocidental	western	
óculos	glasses	
oeste	west	
oficina	repair shop, workshop	
oitenta	eighty	
oito	eight	
oitocentos	eight hundred	
olá	hello	
olho	eye	
oliveira	olive tree	
onde	where	
ontem	yesterday	
onze	eleven	
opção	option	
orelha	ear	
origem	origin	
osso	bone	
ou	or	
ouro	gold	
outono	Autumn	
outro	another	
outubro	October	
ouvido	ear	
ovas	spawn	
ovelha	sheep	
ovo	egg	
P		
padaria	bakery	
padrão	standard	
padre	priest	
padrinho	godfather	
pai	father	
pais	parents	
país	country	
palavra	word	
palmeira	palm tree	
pano	cloth	
pão	bread	
papa	mush	
papelaria	stationary store	
papo	crop	
para	to, for	
para trás	back	
paragem	stop	
pardal	sparrow	

PORTUGUESE	ENGLISH	YOUR LANGUAGE
parecer	to look like, to seem	
parede	wall	
parente	relative	
parte	part, portion	
participação	participation	
partida	departure	
partir	to leave	
páscoa	Easter	
passaporte	passport	
passatempo	hobby	
pastelaria	pastry shop	
pato	duck	
pátria	motherland	
paz	peace	
pé	foot	
peito	chest	
peixe	fish	
peixe-espada	hairtail	
pele	skin	
pensão	boarding house	
pensar	to think	
pequeno	small	
pequeno-almoço	breakfast	
pera	pear	
perante	towards	
percebes	barnacles	
perder	to miss, to loose	
pereira	pear tree	
perfumaria	perfumery	
pergunta	question	
perigo	danger	
permanentemente	permanently	
perna	leg	
pérola	pearl	
perto	near	
peru	turkey	
pesado	heavy	
pescada	hake	
pescoço	neck	
pêssego	peach	
pessoa	person	
piada	joke	
picante	hot, spicy	
pimenta	pepper	
pimento	sweet pepper	
pingo	drop, small coffee with milk (North)	
pinhal	pinewood	
pinheiro	pine tree	
pintura	painting	

PORTUGUESE	ENGLISH	YOUR LANGUAGE
pior	worse	
pirâmide	pyramid	
piripíri	chilli	
piscina	swimming pool	
planície	plain	
plano	flat	
planta	plant	
plástico	plastic	
pó	powder	
pobre	poor	
poder	can	
poesia	poetry	
pois	indeed, yes	
polaco	Polish	
polícia	police	
política	politics	
poluição	polution	
polvo	octopus	
pomba	dove	
pombo	pigeon	
ponte	bridge	
ponto	point	
população	population	
popular	popular	
por	by, for	
porcelana	chinaware	
porco	pig, pork	
porquê	why	
porque	why, because	
porra (slang)	damn, crap	
porta	door	
portanto	so, therefore	
porto	port	
português	Portuguese	
postal	post-card	
pouco	few	
pousada	heritage inn	
praça	square	
praia	beach	
prata	silver	
prato	dish, plate	
prazer	pleasure	
precisar	to need	
prédio	building	
prenda	gift	
preto	black	
previsão	forecast	
primário	primary	
primavera	Spring	
primeiro	first	

PORTUGUESE	ENGLISH	YOUR LANGUAGE
primo	cousin	
problema	trouble, problem	
processo	process	
professor	professor, teacher	
pronto	ready	
pronúncia	pronunciation	
protestante	Protestant	
pudim	pudding	
pulmão	lung	
pulôver	pullover	
puro	pure	
puxar	to pull	

Q

quadro	painting, picture	
qual	which	
qualidade	quality	
qualificador	qualifier	
quantidade	quantity	
quantificador	quantifier	
quanto	how much	
quantos	how many	
quarenta	forty	
quarta-feira	Wednesday	
quarto	bedroom	
quatro	four	
quatrocentos	four hundred	
quê	what	
que	what, that	
queijo	cheese	
quem	who	
quente	hot	
querer	to want	
quieto	quiet	
quilómetro	kilometer	
quimbundo	Kimbundu	
quinhentos	five hundred	
quinta	farm	
quinta-feira	Thursday	
quinto	fifth	
quinze	fifteen	

R

rã	frog	
rádio	radio	
rali	car race	
rapariga	girl	
rapaz	boy	
rápido	fast	
rato	mouse	

PORTUGUESE	ENGLISH	YOUR LANGUAGE
real	real	
realmente	really	
receita	prescription, recipe	
recordação	souvenir	
recorte	cutting	
refeição	meal	
regra	rule	
religião	religion	
relógio	clock, watch	
remédio	healer	
remetente	sender	
rés do chão	groundfloor	
residencial	guest house	
restaurante	restaurant	
retrete	toilet	
revista	magazine	
revolução	revolution	
revolucionário	revolutionary	
ria	estuary	
ribeira	brook	
rico	rich	
rim	kidney	
rio	river	
romeno	Romanian	
rosa	rose	
rótulo	label	
roupa	clothes	
roxo	violet	
rua	street	
russo	Russian	

S

PORTUGUESE	ENGLISH	YOUR LANGUAGE
sábado	Saturday	
saber	to know	
sabonete	soap	
saboroso	tasty	
saco	bag	
sagrado	sacred	
saia	skirt	
saída	exit	
sair	to go out	
sal	salt	
salada	salad	
salsa	parsley	
sandes	sandwich	
sangue	blood	
sanita	toilet	
sanitários	toilets	
santo, santa	saint	
são	saint	

PORTUGUESE	ENGLISH	YOUR LANGUAGE
sapataria	shoe shop	
sapato	shoe	
sapo	toad	
sardinha	sardine	
saúde	health	
se	if	
sé	cathedral	
século	century	
sede	thirst	
segunda-feira	Monday	
segundo	second	
segurança	security	
seguro	safe, insurance	
seis	six	
seiscentos	six hundred	
selo	stamp	
selvagem	wild	
sem	without	
semana	week	
sempre	always	
senhor	gentleman, mister	
senhora	lady, Mrs, Ms	
sentimento	feeling	
sentir	to feel	
ser	to be (more permanent)	
serra	mountain	
sessenta	sixty	
sete	seven	
setecentos	seven hundred	
setembro	September	
setenta	seventy	
seu (masc.)	your, yours, his, her, hers, its	
sexta-feira	Friday	
silva	blackberry bush	
sim	yes	
simpático	nice	
sinal	sign	
só	only	
sobreiro	cork oak	
sobremesa	dessert	
sobrinha	niece	
sobrinho	nephew	
sociedade	society	
socorro	help	
sogra	mother-in-law	
sogro	father-in-law	
sol	sun	
soletração	spelling	
solidão	solitude, loneliness	
solteiro	single	

PORTUGUESE	ENGLISH	YOUR LANGUAGE
sono	sleep	
sopa	soup	
sorte	luck	
sossegado	quiet	
sotaque	accent	
stand	car shop	
suaíli	Swahili	
subida	way up	
submarino	submarine	
sueco	Swedish	
sujo	dirty	
sul	south	
sumo	juice	
supermercado	supermarket	
supositório	suppository	
sutiã	bra	

T

PORTUGUESE	ENGLISH	YOUR LANGUAGE
tá	ok, yes	
taberna	tavern	
talheres	cutlery	
talho	butcher's	
talvez	maybe	
tamanho	size	
tamboril	monkfish	
tangerina	tangerine	
tarde	afternoon, evening before sunset	
tá-se, tasse	cool (slang)	
táxi	taxi	
tchau	bye	
teatro	theater	
tecido	fabric	
teclar	to type (informal)	
telefone	telephone, phone	
telefonema	phone call	
telemóvel	mobile phone	
televisão	television	
temperatura	temperature	
tempestade	storm	
tempo	weather, time	
temporal	storm	
ténis	sneakers	
ter	to have	
terça-feira	Tuesday	
termómetro	thermometer	
terra	land, earth, ground	
tesoura	scissors	
tia	aunt	
tio	uncle	

PORTUGUESE	ENGLISH	YOUR LANGUAGE
toalha	towel	
toilete	toilets	
tomate	tomato	
torcer	to bend	
torneira	tap	
torrada	toast	
tosse	cough	
tosta	grilled bread	
totalmente	totally	
toucinho	bacon	
tourada	bull fight	
touro	bull	
trabalhador	worker	
trabalho	job, work	
trânsito	traffic	
transporte	transportation	
trás	behind, back	
tratamento	treatment	
travessa	tray	
travesseiro	throw pillow	
três	three	
treze	thirteen	
trezentos	three hundred	
trigo	wheat	
trinta	thirty	
tripas	guts	
triste	sad	
trouxa	pack	
trovoada	thunderstorm	
truta	trout	
t-shirt	t-shirt	
tuga (slang)	Portuguese	
turco	Turkish	

U

ucraniano	Ukrainian	
último	last	
um	one, a, an	
unha	nail	
único	single	
universidade	university	
urgente	urgent	
urso	bear	
usar	to use	
utilidade	utility	
uva	grape	

V

vaca	cow, beef	
vacina	vaccine	

| --- | --- | --- |
vale	valley	
vaso	vase	
vassoura	broom	
vegetal	vegetable	
vela	candle	
velho	old	
vender	to sell	
vento	wind	
ver	to see	
verão	Summer	
verbo	verb	
verdade	truth	
verde	green, unripe	
vermelho	red	
vestido	dress	
viagem	travel, trip	
vida	life	
videira	vine	
vidro	glass	
vila	town	
vindima	vintage	
vinha	vineyard	
vinho	wine	
vinho branco	white wine	
vinho tinto	red wine	
vinho verde	unripe-grape wine	
vinte	twenty	
vir	to come	
viúva	widow	
viúvo	widower	
vizinho	neighbour	
você	you (singular, formal)	
vocês	you (plural)	
vodca	vodka	
volta	return	
voltar	to turn back, to come back, to return	
vomitar	to throw up	
vós	you (plural, old)	
whisky	whisky	
xadrez	chess	
xaile	shawl	
xarope	syrup	
xilofone	xylophone	
zebra	zebra	
zero	zero	
zulo	Zulu	

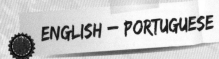

ENGLISH – PORTUGUESE

ENGLISH	PORTUGUESE	YOUR LANGUAGE
A		
a, an	um, uma	
abbot	abade	
accent	sotaque	
accident	acidente	
action	ação	
address	morada	
address, greetings	cumprimentos	
addressee	destinatário	
after	depois	
afternoon	tarde	
age	idade	
ahead	em frente	
air	ar	
airplane	avião	
airport	aeroporto	
albatross	albatroz, alcatraz	
alcohol	álcool	
almond	amêndoa	
already	já	
aluminum	alumínio	
always	sempre	
ambulance	ambulância	
American	americano, gringo (slang)	
and	e	
angel	anjo	
animal	animal	
another	outro	
ant	formiga	
apple	maçã	
April	abril	
Arab, Arabic	árabe	
architect	arquiteto	
area	área	
arm	braço	
arrival	chegada	
art	arte	
artist	artista	
ash	cinza	
at	em	
atheist	ateu	
athletics	atletismo	
ATM	multibanco	
attention	atenção	
attitude	atitude	
August	agosto	
aunt	tia	

ENGLISH	PORTUGUESE	YOUR LANGUAGE
Autumn	outono	
avenue	avenida	
away	embora	

B

ENGLISH	PORTUGUESE	YOUR LANGUAGE
baby	bebé	
back	costas, trás, para trás	
backpack	mochila	
bacon	bacon, toucinho	
bad	mau	
badly	mal	
bag	saco	
bakery	padaria	
ball	bola, baile	
bamboo	bambu	
banana	banana	
band	banda	
bank	banco, margem	
bar	bar	
barber's	barbeiro	
barnacles	percebes	
baroque	barroco	
basket	cesto	
basketball	basquetebol	
bathroom	casa de banho	
bathtub	banheira	
beach	praia	
bean	feijão	
bear	urso	
beard	barba	
beautiful	bonito	
beauty	beleza	
because	porque	
bed	cama	
bedroom	quarto	
bee	abelha	
beef	vaca	
beer	cerveja, caneca (large draught), fino (regular draught, North), imperial (regular draught)	
beer house	cervejaria	
before	antes	
behind	atrás, trás	
Belgian	belga	
belly	barriga	
belt	cinto	
better	melhor	
between	entre	
bicycle	bicicleta	

ENGLISH	PORTUGUESE	YOUR LANGUAGE
bidet	bidé	
big	grande	
bigger	maior	
bill	conta	
billiards	bilhar	
biscuit	bolacha	
bishop	bispo	
bit	bocado	
black	preto	
black cherry	ginja	
blackberry bush	silva	
blanket	cobertor	
bloke	gajo	
blond	louro	
blood	sangue	
blouse	blusa	
blue	azul	
boarding house	pensão	
boat	barco	
body	corpo	
boiled	cozido	
bone	osso	
book	livro	
bookshop	livraria	
boot	bota	
boredom	chatice	
bottle	garrafa	
box	caixa	
boy	rapaz	
boyfriend	namorado	
bra	sutiã	
brain	cérebro	
brandy	aguardente, bagaço	
Brazilian	brazuca (slang)	
bread	pão	
breakfast	pequeno-almoço	
bridge	ponte	
Brit	bife (slang)	
bronze	bronze	
brook	ribeira	
broom	vassoura	
brother	irmão	
brother-in-law	cunhado	
brown	castanho	
brunette	moreno	
Buddhist	budista	
building	edifício, prédio	
bulb	lâmpada	
bull	touro	
bull fight	tourada	

ENGLISH	PORTUGUESE	YOUR LANGUAGE
bus	autocarro	
but	mas	
butcher's	talho	
butter	manteiga	
butterfly	borboleta	
buying	compra	
by	por	
bye	tchau, adeus	

C

ENGLISH	PORTUGUESE	YOUR LANGUAGE
cabbage	couve	
cabbage sprout	grelo	
café	café	
cake	bolo	
calendar	calendário	
call	chamada	
camel	camelo	
camping	campismo	
can	poder	
candle	vela	
cantaloupe	meloa	
Capeverdean	cabo-verdiano	
car	carro	
car race	rali	
car shop	stand	
care	cuidado	
carnation	cravo	
carnival	carnaval	
carpenter	carpinteiro	
carrot	cenoura	
cart	carroça	
cartoon	caricatura	
cashew	caju	
cashier	caixa	
cat	gato	
cathedral	catedral, sé	
cellar	adega	
century	século	
cereal	cereal	
certainty	certeza	
chair	cadeira	
chapel	capela	
cheap	barato	
check	controlo	
cheese	queijo	
chemist	farmácia	
cherry	cereja	
chess	xadrez	
chest	peito	
chestnut	castanha, castanheiro	

ENGLISH	PORTUGUESE	YOUR LANGUAGE
chicken	frango	
chief	chefe	
child	criança	
chilli	piripíri	
chinaware	porcelana	
chocolate	chocolate	
christening	batizado	
Christian	cristão	
Christmas	natal	
church	igreja	
cigarette	cigarro	
cinema	cinema	
circus	circo	
city	cidade	
clam	amêijoa	
class	classe	
clay	barro	
cleaning	limpeza	
clock	relógio	
cloth	pano	
clothes	roupa	
cloud	nuvem	
cloudy	nublado	
club	clube	
coach	camioneta	
cobra	cobra	
cock	galo, caralho (slang)	
coconut	coco	
cod	bacalhau	
coffee	café, café duplo (large espresso), bica (regular espresso), carioca (light black), cimbalino (regular espresso, North), galão (large with milk), garoto (small with milk), italiana (small espresso), meia de leite (regular with milk), pingo (small with milk, North)	
coin	moeda	
cold	frio, constipação	
colleague	colega	
collection	coleção	
colour	cor	
comics	banda desenhada	
company	companhia	
competition	competição	
completly	completamente	
computer	computador	

ENGLISH	PORTUGUESE	YOUR LANGUAGE
communism	comunismo	
concert	concerto	
construction	construção	
contrary	contrário	
control	controlo	
convent	convento	
conversation, talk	conversa	
cool	fresco, fixe (slang), tá-se (slang)	
copper	cobre	
cork	cortiça	
cork oak	sobreiro	
corn	milho	
corridor	corredor	
cotton	algodão	
cough	tosse	
country	país	
countryside	campo	
couple	casal	
cousin	primo	
cow	vaca	
crab	caranguejo	
crap	porra (slang)	
cream	creme, natas	
crop	papo	
crossroad	cruzamento	
crystal	cristal	
culture	cultura	
cup	chávena	
customs	alfândega	
cute	giro	
cutlery	talheres	
cutting	recorte	
Czech	checo	

D

daisy	malmequer	
dam	barragem	
damn	porra (slang)	
dance	dança	
danger	perigo	
Danish	dinamarquês	
date	data	
daughter	filha	
daughter-in-law	nora	
day	dia	
death	morte	
debit card	multibanco	
december	dezembro	
democracy	democracia	

ENGLISH	PORTUGUESE	YOUR LANGUAGE
departure	partida	
desk	balcão, guiché	
dessert	sobremesa	
destination	destino	
development	desenvolvimento	
dialogue	diálogo	
dice	dado	
dictatorship	ditadura	
dictionary	dicionário	
difference	diferença	
different	diferente	
difficult	difícil	
difficulty	dificuldade	
dinner	jantar	
direct	direto	
direction	direção	
dirty	sujo	
disco	discoteca	
discovery	descobrimento	
dish	prato	
distance	distância	
doctor	doutor, médico	
doctor's appointment	consulta	
document	documento	
dog	cão	
donkey	burro	
door	porta	
doubt	dúvida	
dove	pomba	
dragon	dragão	
drawing	desenho	
dress	vestido	
dribble	baba	
drink	bebida	
drop	pingo	
drum	batuque	
duck	pato	

E

eagle	águia	
ear	orelha, ouvido	
early	cedo	
earth	terra	
east	este, leste	
Easter	páscoa	
easy	fácil	
egg	ovo	
eight	oito	
eight hundred	oitocentos	
eighteen	dezoito	

ENGLISH	PORTUGUESE	YOUR LANGUAGE
eighty	oitenta	
elephant	elefante	
eletricista	electrician	
eleven	onze	
emergency	emergência	
empire	império	
engineer	engenheiro	
English	inglês	
entrance	entrada	
envelope	envelope	
environment	ambiente	
essentially	essencialmente	
estuary	ria, estuário	
eucalyptus	eucalipto	
evening	tarde (before sunset), noite (after sunset)	
examination	exame	
excuse	licença	
exhibition	exposição	
exit	saída	
expense	despesa	
expensive	caro	
extraordinary	extraordinário	
eye	olho	

F

fabric	tecido	
face	cara	
factory	fábrica	
fair	feira	
family	família	
family name	apelido	
far	longe	
farm	quinta	
farmer	agricultor	
fascism	fascismo	
fast	rápido	
fat	gordo	
father	pai	
father-in-law	sogro	
favour	favor	
fear	medo	
February	fevereiro	
feeling	sentimento	
fetish	fetiche	
fever	febre	
few	pouco	
fiancé	noivo	
fiber	fibra	
field	campo	

ENGLISH	PORTUGUESE	YOUR LANGUAGE
fifteen	quinze	
fifth	quinto	
fifty	cinquenta	
fig	figo	
film	filme	
finally	finalmente	
finger	dedo	
Finnish	finlandês	
fire	fogo	
firm	empresa	
first	primeiro	
fish	peixe	
five	cinco	
five hundred	quinhentos	
flat	plano	
flesh	carne	
flounder	linguado	
flour	farinha	
flower	flor	
flu	gripe	
fly	mosca	
fog	nevoeiro	
food	comida	
foot	pé	
football	futebol	
for	para, por	
forecast	previsão	
foreign, foreigner	estrangeiro	
foreigner	camone (slang)	
fork	garfo	
forty	quarenta	
foundation	fundação	
fountain	fonte	
four	quatro	
four hundred	quatrocentos	
fourteen	catorze	
freedom	liberdade	
French	francês, franciú (slang)	
friday	sexta-feira	
fried	frito	
friend	amigo	
frog	rã	
front	frente	
frost	geada	
fruit	fruta (general), fruto (single)	
fuck it	foda-se	
fun	brincadeira	
future	futuro	

ENGLISH	PORTUGUESE	YOUR LANGUAGE
G		
Galician	galego	
game	jogo	
garage	garagem	
garbage	lixo	
garden	jardim	
garlic	alho	
gas station	bomba de gasolina	
general	geral	
gentleman	senhor	
German	alemão	
gift	prenda	
gin	gin	
gipsy	cigano	
girl	rapariga	
girlfriend	namorada	
glass	vidro, copo	
glasses	óculos	
glue	cola	
goal	golo	
goat	cabra	
goatling	cabrito	
god	deus	
godfather	padrinho	
godmother	madrinha	
going	ida	
gold	ouro	
good	bom, boa	
goodbye	adeus	
government	governo	
grammar	gramática	
granddaughter	neta	
grandfather	avô	
grandmother	avó	
grandparents	avós	
grandson	neto	
grape	uva	
Greek	grego	
green	verde	
grey	cinzento	
grief	desgosto	
grilled	grelhado	
grilled bread	tosta	
grocer's	mercearia	
ground	terra	
groundfloor	rés do chão	
guest house	residencial	
guide	guia	
Guinean	guineense	
guts	tripas	

ENGLISH	PORTUGUESE	YOUR LANGUAGE
guy	gajo (slang)	
gymnastics	ginástica	

H

ENGLISH	PORTUGUESE	YOUR LANGUAGE
habit	costume	
hair	cabelo	
hairdresser	cabeleireiro	
hairtail	peixe-espada	
hake	pescada	
half	metade	
hand	mão	
handball	andebol	
handkerchief	lenço	
happiness	alegria	
happy	alegre	
hare	lebre	
hashish	haxe (slang)	
hat	chapéu	
he	ele	
head	cabeça	
healer	remédio	
health	saúde	
heart	coração	
heat	calor	
heating	aquecimento	
heaven	céu	
heavy	pesado	
Hebrew	hebraico	
heck (slang)	caraças	
hell (slang)	fogo (slang)	
hello	olá	
help	ajuda, socorro	
hen	galinha	
her, hers	sua (fem.)	
here	aqui	
heritage inn	pousada	
hill	monte	
Hindi	hindi	
hippopotamus	hipopótamo	
his	seu (masc.)	
history	história	
hobby	passatempo	
holiday	feriado	
holidays	férias	
honey	mel	
horn	corno	
horse	cavalo	
horse mackerel	carapau	
hospital	hospital	
hot	quente, picante	

ENGLISH	PORTUGUESE	YOUR LANGUAGE
hotdog	cachorro	
hotel	hotel	
hour	hora	
house	casa	
how	como	
how many	quantos	
how much	quanto	
hug	abraço	
human	humano	
humidity	humidade	
hundred	cem, cento	
hungarian	húngaro	
hunger	fome	
hungry	com fome	
hunting	caça	
husband	marido	

I	eu	
Iberian	ibérico	
ice	gelo	
ice cream	gelado	
if	se	
ill	doente	
illness	doença	
important	importante	
impossible	impossível	
in	em	
indeed	pois	
infinite	infinito	
injection	injeção	
inn	estalagem	
inside	dentro	
insurance	seguro	
intention	intenção	
interesting	interessante	
invitation	convite	
it	ele, ela	
Italian	italiano	
its	seu (masc.)	

jacket	casaco	
january	janeiro	
Japanese	japonês	
Jesuit	jesuíta	
Jew, Jewish	judeu	
job	emprego, trabalho	
joint (slang)	charro	

ENGLISH	PORTUGUESE	YOUR LANGUAGE
joke	piada, anedota	
journalist	jornalista	
joy	alegria	
judge	juiz	
juice	sumo	
July	julho	
June	junho	
justice	justiça	

K

key	chave	
kidney	rim	
kilometer	quilómetro	
kimbundu	quimbundo	
kiss	beijo	
kitchen	cozinha	
knee	joelho	
knife	faca	

L

label	rótulo	
lady	senhora, dona	
lake	lago	
lamb	carneiro	
lamp	candeeiro	
lamprey	lampreia	
land	terra	
language	língua	
last	último	
late	tarde	
later	logo, mais tarde	
Latin	latim	
laughter	gargalhada	
law	lei	
lawyer	advogado	
leader	líder	
left	esquerda	
leg	perna	
lemon	limão	
leonese	leonês	
letter	letra, carta	
lettuce	alface	
liberty	liberdade	
lie	mentira	
life	vida	
lift	elevador	
light	leve	
likewise	igualmente	
line	linha, fila	
linen	linho	

ENGLISH	PORTUGUESE	YOUR LANGUAGE
lion	leão	
liter	litro	
literature	literatura	
Lithuanian	lituano	
liver	fígado	
lobster	lagosta	
loneliness	solidão	
love	amor	
luck	sorte	
luggage	bagagem	
lunch	almoço	
lung	pulmão	
lyrics	letra	

M

ENGLISH	PORTUGUESE	YOUR LANGUAGE
magazine	revista	
mail	correio	
Malay	malaio	
man	homem	
Mandarin	mandarim	
mango	manga	
many	muitos	
map	mapa	
March	março	
maritime	marítimo	
market	mercado	
marmalade	marmelada	
mass	missa	
match	jogo	
material	material	
mattress	colchão	
maximum	máximo	
May	maio	
maybe	talvez	
me	eu	
meal	refeição	
means	meio	
meat	carne	
mechanic	mecânico	
meeting	encontro	
melon	melão	
member of parliament	deputado	
menu	menu	
middle	meio	
milk	leite	
mill	moinho	
million	milhão	
mine	meu (masc.)	
minister	ministro	

ENGLISH	PORTUGUESE	YOUR LANGUAGE
minute	minuto	
Mirandese	mirandês	
mirror	espelho	
mister	senhor	
mobile	móvel	
molasses	melaço	
moment	momento	
Monday	segunda-feira	
monetary	monetário	
money	dinheiro	
money exchange	câmbio	
monkey	macaco	
monkfish	tamboril	
month	mês	
monument	monumento	
moon	lua	
more	mais	
morning	manhã	
mosquito	mosquito	
mother	mãe	
mother-in-law	sogra	
motherland	pátria	
motorbike	mota	
mountain	serra, montanha	
mouse	rato	
mousse	baba (old)	
mouth	boca, foz	
Mozarabic	moçárabe	
Mrs	senhora	
much	muito	
museum	museu	
mush	papa	
music	música	
Muslim	muçulmano	
my	meu (masc.)	

N

nail	unha	
name	nome	
napkin	guardanapo	
natural	natural	
navy	marinha	
near	perto	
neck	pescoço	
neighbour	vizinho	
neighbourhood	bairro	
nephew	sobrinho	
never	nunca	
new	novo	
news	notícia(s)	

ENGLISH	PORTUGUESE	YOUR LANGUAGE
newspaper	jornal	
next to	ao lado de	
nice	simpático	
niece	sobrinha	
night	noite	
nine	nove	
nine hundred	novecentos	
nineteen	dezanove	
ninety	noventa	
no	não	
noise	barulho	
north	norte	
nose	nariz	
not	não	
notebook	caderno	
nothing	nada	
November	novembro	
now	agora	
number	número	
nun	freira	
nurse	enfermeiro	
nut	noz	

O

oak	carvalho	
obviously	obviamente	
October	outubro	
octopus	polvo	
of	de	
office	escritório	
ok	ok, tá	
old	velho	
olive	azeitona	
olive oil	azeite	
olive tree	oliveira	
on	em	
one	um	
onion	cebola	
only	só	
option	opção	
or	ou	
orange	laranja, cor de laranja	
order	encomenda	
origin	origem	
outside	fora	
owner	dono	
ox	boi	

P

pack	trouxa	

ENGLISH	PORTUGUESE	YOUR LANGUAGE
pain	dor	
painting	pintura, quadro	
palm tree	palmeira	
pants	cuecas	
paragem	stop	
parcel	encomenda	
parents	pais	
parsley	salsa	
part	parte	
participation	participação	
party	festa	
passport	passaporte	
pasta	massa	
pastry shop	pastelaria	
pastime	divertimento	
patient	doente	
peace	paz	
peach	pêssego	
peanut	amendoim	
pear	pera	
pear tree	pereira	
pearl	pérola	
pen	caneta	
pencil	lápis	
people	gente	
pepper	pimenta	
perfumery	perfumaria	
permanently	permanentemente	
person	pessoa	
phone	telefone	
photo	fotografia	
phrase	expressão	
picture	quadro, figura	
pig	porco	
pigeon	pombo	
piglet	leitão	
pill	comprimido	
pillow	almofada	
pine tree	pinheiro	
pineapple	ananás	
pinewood	pinhal	
pink	cor-de-rosa	
plain	planície	
plane	avião	
plant	planta	
plastic	plástico	
plate	prato	
platform	linha	
please	se faz favor, por favor	
pleasure	prazer	

ENGLISH	PORTUGUESE	YOUR LANGUAGE
plum	ameixa	
pocket	bolso	
poetry	poesia	
point	ponto	
police	polícia	
Polish	polaco	
politics	política	
polution	poluição	
poor	pobre	
popular	popular	
population	população	
pork	porco	
port	porto	
portion	parte	
Portuguese	português, tuga (slang)	
Portuguese sign language	língua gestual portuguesa (LGP)	
post office	correios	
postbox	marco do correio	
post-card	postal	
potato	batata	
pottery	cerâmica	
powder	pó	
prescription	receita	
press	imprensa	
priest	padre	
primary	primário	
private school	colégio	
problem	problema	
process	processo	
professor	professor	
pronunciation	pronúncia	
protestant	protestante	
pudding	pudim	
pullover	pulôver	
puppet	boneco	
pure	puro	
purse	mala	
pyramid	pirâmide	

Q

ENGLISH	PORTUGUESE	YOUR LANGUAGE
qualifier	qualificador	
quality	qualidade	
quantifier	quantificador	
quantity	quantidade	
question	pergunta	
queue	fila	
quiet	quieto, sossegado	
quince	marmelo	

ENGLISH	PORTUGUESE	YOUR LANGUAGE
R		
rabbit	coelho	
radio	rádio	
rain	chuva	
raincoat	gabardine	
reading	leitura	
ready	pronto	
real	real	
really	realmente	
recipe	receita	
record	disco	
record player	gira-discos	
red	encarnado, vermelho, tinto	
relative	parente	
religion	religião	
repair shop	oficina	
reservoir	barragem	
resourcefulness	desenrascanço (slang)	
restaurant	restaurante	
return	volta	
revolution	revolução	
revolutionary	revolucionário	
rice	arroz	
rich	rico	
right	direita	
river	rio	
road	estrada	
roasted	assado	
Roman Catholic	católico	
Romani	cigano	
Romanian	romeno	
rose	rosa	
rubber	borracha	
rule	regra	
Russian	russo	
rye	centeio	
S		
sacred	sagrado	
sad	triste	
safe	seguro	
sailor	marinheiro	
saint	santo, santa, são	
salad	salada	
salt	sal	
same	igual	
sandwich	sandes	
sardine	sardinha	
Saturday	sábado	
schedule	horário	

ENGLISH	PORTUGUESE	YOUR LANGUAGE
school	escola	
science	ciência	
scissors	tesoura	
screen	biombo	
sea	mar	
sea smell	maresia	
sea sound	marulhar	
seafood	marisco	
seafood restaurant	marisqueira	
seagull	gaivota	
seaside	beira-mar	
season	estação	
second	segundo	
security	segurança	
sender	remetente	
sentence	frase	
September	setembro	
sessenta	sixty	
seven	sete	
seven hundred	setecentos	
seventeen	dezassete	
seventy	setenta	
shampoo	champô	
shape	forma	
shawl	xaile	
she	ela	
sheep	ovelha	
sheet	lençol	
shirt	camisa	
shit (slang)	merda	
shoe	sapato	
shoe shop	sapataria	
shop	loja	
shopping	compras	
shopping center	centro comercial	
short	baixo	
shorts	calções	
show	espectáculo	
shower	chuveiro, aguaceiro	
shrimp	camarão	
sick	doente	
sign	sinal	
signature	assinatura	
silver	prata	
since	desde	
single	solteiro, único	
sister	irmã	
sister-in-law	cunhada	
six	seis	
six hundred	seiscentos	

ENGLISH	PORTUGUESE	YOUR LANGUAGE
sixteen	dezasseis	
size	tamanho	
skin	pele	
skirt	saia	
sky	céu	
sleep	sono	
sleeve	manga	
slim	magro	
slow	devagar; lento	
small	pequeno	
small square	largo	
smell	cheiro	
snack (in mid afternoon)	lanche	
snail	caracol	
snake	cobra	
sneakers	ténis	
sneeze	espirro	
snow	neve	
so	portanto	
soap	sabonete	
society	sociedade	
soft	mole	
solitude	solidão	
son	filho	
song	canção	
son-in-law	genro	
sorry	desculpe	
soup	sopa	
south	sul	
souvenir	recordação, lembrança	
spanish	espanhol	
sparrow	pardal	
spelling	soletração	
spicy	picante	
spider	aranha	
spirit	espírito	
spoon	colher	
sport	desporto	
spawn	ovas	
Spring	primavera	
square	praça	
squid	lula	
stadium	estádio	
stair	escada	
stamp	selo	
standard	padrão	
state	estado	
station	estação	
stationary store	papelaria	

ENGLISH	PORTUGUESE	YOUR LANGUAGE
statue	estátua	
steak	bife	
steel	aço	
stomach	estômago	
store	armazém	
storm	tempestade, temporal	
story	história	
strawberry	morango	
street	rua	
street market	feira	
strike	greve	
strong	forte	
student	estudante	
style	estilo	
subject	assunto	
submarine	submarino	
sugar	açúcar	
suit	fato	
suitcase	mala	
Summer	verão	
sun	sol	
Sunday	domingo	
supermarket	supermercado	
suppository	supositório	
Swahili	suaíli	
swallow	andorinha	
sweater	camisola	
Swedish	sueco	
sweet	doce	
sweet pepper	pimento	
swimming	natação	
swimming pool	piscina	
syrup	xarope	

T

ENGLISH	PORTUGUESE	YOUR LANGUAGE
table	mesa	
tag	etiqueta	
tall, loud	alto	
tangerine	tangerina	
tap	torneira	
tasty	saboroso	
tavern	taberna	
taxi	táxi	
tea	chá	
tea (in the evening)	lanche	
teacher	professor	
team	equipa	
teenager	jovem	
telephone	telefone	
television	televisão	

ENGLISH	PORTUGUESE	YOUR LANGUAGE
temperature	temperatura	
ten	dez	
thanks	obrigado	
that	isso (near), aquilo (far), que	
the	o, os, a, as	
theater	teatro	
there	aí (near), ali (far)	
therefore	portanto	
thermometer	termómetro	
they	eles, elas	
thick	grosso	
thin	fino	
thirst	sede	
thirsty	com sede	
thirteen	treze	
thirty	trinta	
this	isto	
thousand	mil	
thread	fio	
three	três	
three hundred	trezentos	
throw pillow	travesseiro	
thunder storm	trovoada	
Thursday	quinta-feira	
ticket	bilhete	
ticket office	bilheteira	
ticket window	guiché	
tide	maré	
tie	gravata	
time	tempo	
timetable	horário	
tin	estanho	
tip	gorjeta	
to	para, a	
to be	ser (more permanent), estar (less permanent)	
to bend	torcer	
to call	chamar	
to catch	apanhar	
to come	vir	
to come back	voltar	
to cost	custar	
to die	morrer	
to do	fazer	
to feel	sentir	
to find	achar	
to forget	esquecer	
to give	dar	
to globalize	globalizar	
to go	ir	

ENGLISH	PORTUGUESE	YOUR LANGUAGE
to go out	sair	
to have	ter, haver	
to implement	implementar	
to know	conhecer, saber	
to land in the moon	alunar	
to land on water	amarar	
to leave	partir	
to like	gostar	
to look like	parecer	
to loose	perder	
to love	amar	
to miss	perder	
to need	precisar	
to pull	puxar	
to push	empurrar	
to return	voltar	
to revel	desbundar (slang)	
to say	dizer	
to see	ver	
to seem	parecer	
to sell	vender	
to send	mandar	
to show	mostrar	
to sing	cantar	
to speak	falar	
to stay	ficar	
to swallow	engolir	
to think	pensar	
to throw up	vomitar	
to turn back	voltar	
to type	teclar (informal)	
to understand	compreender	
to use	usar	
to wait	esperar	
to walk	andar	
to want	querer	
to worship	adorar	
to write	escrever	
toad	sapo	
toast	torrada	
today	hoje	
toe	dedo	
toilet	sanita, retrete	
toilets	toilete, lavabos, sanitários	
tomato	tomate	
tomorrow	amanhã	
tongue	língua	
tooth	dente	
totally	totalmente	
towards	perante	

ENGLISH	PORTUGUESE	YOUR LANGUAGE
towel	toalha	
town	vila	
trader	comerciante	
traffic	trânsito	
train	comboio	
tram	elétrico	
transportation	transporte	
travel	viagem	
tray	travessa	
treatment	tratamento	
tree	árvore	
tricky	complicado	
trip	viagem	
trouble	problema	
trousers	calças	
trout	truta	
truck	camião	
truth	verdade	
t-shirt	t-shirt	
tsunami	maremoto	
Tuesday	terça-feira	
tuna	atum	
turkey	peru	
Turkish	turco	
twelve	doze	
twenty	vinte	
two	dois	
two hundred	duzentos	

U

ENGLISH	PORTUGUESE	YOUR LANGUAGE
ugly	feio	
Ukrainian	ucraniano	
uncle	tio	
underground, tube	metro	
unemployment	desemprego	
university	universidade	
unripe	verde	
untill	até	
urgent	urgente	
utility	utilidade	

V

ENGLISH	PORTUGUESE	YOUR LANGUAGE
vaccine	vacina	
valley	vale	
vase	vaso	
vegetable	vegetal, legume	
verb	verbo	
very	muito, bué (slang)	
village	aldeia	
vine	videira	

ENGLISH	PORTUGUESE	YOUR LANGUAGE
vineyard	vinha	
vintage	vindima	
violet	roxo	
vodka	vodca	

W

ENGLISH	PORTUGUESE	YOUR LANGUAGE
waiting	espera	
wall	parede	
wallet	carteira	
walnut	noz	
war	guerra	
wardrobe	armário	
washbasin	lavatório	
watch	relógio	
water	água	
watermelon	melancia	
way	caminho	
way down	descida	
way up	subida	
we	nós	
weak	fraco	
weather	tempo	
wedding	casamento	
Wednesday	quarta-feira	
weed (slang)	erva	
week	semana	
weekend	fim de semana	
well	bem	
west	oeste	
western	ocidental	
what	quê, que	
wheat	trigo	
where	onde	
which	qual	
while	enquanto	
whisky	whisky	
white	branco	
who	quem	
why	porquê, porque	
wide	largo	
widow	viúva	
widower	viúvo	
wife	mulher	
wild	selvagem	
wind	vento	
window	janela	
wine	vinho	
Winter	inverno	
witchcraft	feitiço	
with	com	

ENGLISH	PORTUGUESE	YOUR LANGUAGE
without	sem	
wolf	lobo	
woman	mulher	
wood	madeira	
wool	lã	
word	palavra	
work	trabalho	
worker	trabalhador	
workshop	oficina	
worse	pior	
wound	ferida	

X

xylophone	xilofone	

Y

year	ano	
yellow	amarelo	
yes	sim, tá, pois	
yesterday	ontem	
you	você (singular, formal), vocês (plural), vós (plural, old)	
your, yours	seu (masc.)	

Z

zebra	zebra	
zero	zero	
Zulu	zulo	

Samples

**Phrases, sentences, tags,
labels, tickets,
cuttings, drawings**
*Frases, etiquetas, marcas,
bilhetes, recortes,
desenhos*

229